LIONESSES

ABDULLAH ABDULLAH

LIONESSES
GAMECHANGERS

First published by Pitch Publishing, 2023

Pitch Publishing
9 Donnington Park,
85 Birdham Road,
Chichester,
West Sussex,
PO20 7AJ
www.pitchpublishing.co.uk
info@pitchpublishing.co.uk

A CIP catalogue record is available for this book from the British Library.

ISBN 978 1 80150 433 1

Typesetting and origination by Pitch Publishing

Printed and bound in Great Britain by TJ Books, Padstow

Contents

To Mum, Nunes, and Dad for their unwavering support, and to Domagoj, Mia, Om, Charlotte, and Willie; thanks for believing in me even when I stopped believing in myself.

Foreword

ONLY A handful of the nation would have heard of Leah Williamson a year ago, and even less would have known Beth Mead, but fast forward to today and the pair are brandished on billboards, across the sides of buses and train stations, and are fast on their way, if they aren't already, to becoming household names.

On 31 July 2022, the Lionesses made history when they defeated eight-time champions Germany and won the Euros. From the tribal echoes of 'Toone' and the raw emotion that radiated far beyond the arch of Wembley, to Chloe Kelly's iconic celebration and the 11-minute corner flag affair, the final could not have been written any better.

This, however, was not the first time England have been within touching distance of a major trophy – they have come close before. In 1984 they reached the final of their inaugural Women's Euros under the coaching of Martin Reagan, yet were ultimately beaten by Sweden on penalties. Three years later they reached the semi-finals, where they were undone by Sweden once again.

In total, England have reached both the semi-finals and the final of the Euros three times each. On the world stage they have been equally as vocal. England made it to the quarter-finals of the 1995, 2007, and 2011 World Cups under Ted Copeland and Hope Powell respectively. They then went on to reach the semi-finals of the past two World Cups, under Mark Sampson in 2015 and most recently Phil Neville in 2019, losing to Japan and the USA respectively.

Only one woman has ever managed to get us over the line: Sarina Wiegman. After her introduction to the national team in September 2021, the impact the former Dutch midfielder had on the squad was felt almost immediately. The tactical minds of Wiegman and her assistant, Arjan Veurink, have worked wonders but there is a greater principle that courses deep through her leadership.

For a long time, the Lionesses were down and out. After their defeat to the USA in 2019, England were steadily slipping with a series of muddled and lacklustre displays. The frustration with their performances was shared within the squad itself and their supporters, and confidence was dwindling on both sides of the touchline. This was a team made up of gourmet ingredients but the recipe was all wrong.

Wiegman arrived and quickly re-established order. She made it her business to meet and hold discussions with every player, she set out clear expectations and raised standards, she ensured that every member of the squad felt valued, and worked to vastly improve individual and collective morale. Possibly the greatest example of the environment Wiegman has cultivated is seen in a clip of Bethany England on the final whistle at Wembley. England, despite not playing a single minute of the tournament, was the first player to run on to the pitch and embrace Wiegman, which gives a clear indication of the respect between player and coach.

This unity is partly what has led the nation to fall in love with the Lionesses. While this book largely focuses on the football, this opening section offers the opportunity to briefly touch upon other revolutionary repercussions of the summer.

The word 'inspiration' is thrown around a lot in women's football; 'inspiring girls and boys up and down the country' is usually the obligatory phrase used by reporters to sign off their segments on the news. However, to not mention the effect the Lionesses have had within this publication would be a disservice to their ongoing achievements.

The truth of the matter is the Lionesses do stir something inside. If they didn't, we wouldn't be here – me, writing this foreword, and you reading it. So although we should be careful not to romanticise too much, the Lionesses must be acknowledged and earnestly thanked for their impact off the pitch. For opening conversations, igniting new passions, for encouraging acceptance, and propelling change. They *have* inspired girls and boys up and down the country, they *have* inspired a generation, they *have* inspired people like me.

Growing up, I was always a football fan who loved nothing more than kick-abouts in the garden. I eagerly awaited afternoons in the local sports shop to pick out new boots. I took an interest in the national side in particular and a large amount of my childhood was spent in an England kit. I have vivid memories of playing football on the playground at lunchtimes alongside other girls in primary school and was lucky enough to have been taken under the wing of the one teacher who took it upon herself to build a girls' football team. While football for girls at this age was never actively encouraged, it was not discouraged either.

However, when I moved on to secondary school, this all stopped. PE lessons were split; girls were to play netball and to practise gymnastics, boys were to play football and rugby, and that was that. Despite numerous requests from several students to form a girls' team, by the time I'd reached Year 9 any hope was long gone. The promise was always there but the execution never came through.

I bring this up not for sympathy, but because for girls this was, and in many cases still is, the norm. Thankfully this is now changing. The Lionesses have jump-started a slow-burning movement and are driving it home with public activism such as the Let Girls Play campaign spearheaded by Lotte Wubben-Moy.

Many of those who work within the world of women's football have been advocating for this sort of visibility for years, and after first watching the Lionesses in the 2019 World Cup, I knew I needed to contribute to this cause. I knew I needed to bring eyes to the players, clubs, and leagues of the women's game with the same affection and dedication their male counterparts receive. It is the reason I started writing about the game and designing women's football graphics, and subsequently went on to found the dedicated platform On Her Side.

I describe On Her Side as my own personal 'thank you' to the Lionesses; they rekindled a love that was lost along the way. But further than this I credit On

Her Side with new passion, new experiences, and new friends; in fact, it was through sharing this work online that I first came across the articles of tactical analyst Abdullah Abdullah.

Abdullah is the perfect person to help us not only relive the dream of the summer, but to understand how the Lionesses pulled off what probably should have been unthinkable. Throughout this book Abdullah offers insights into the nuances of Wiegman's tactical choices through detailed accounts that will appeal to both the beginner and the expert.

The landscape of women's football and women's sport is shifting and it is works such as this by Abdullah and his previous titles, *Queens of Europe: Olympique Lyonnais Feminin* and *Europe's Next Powerhouse? The Evolution of Chelsea Under Emma Hayes*, that are supporting this change with the tangible material and legitimate expertise it deserves.

But for now, we can take a moment to celebrate. Chloe Kelly is forever inked on the skin of many, Keira Walsh has established herself as one of England's greatest exports and 'The Russo' has back-heeled its way on to Sunday league pitches and I, for one, am so glad their stories are finally being told.

Charlotte Stacey
Founder of On Her Side

Preface

'So when you have made a decision, then put your trust in Allah.' – Surah Al Imran (3:159)

Alhamdullilah

I DIDN'T ever think I'd be writing one book in my lifetime, let alone three, but here we are. Believe it or not, if you're reading this then you're reading my third in a trilogy of women's football tactics books. Truth be told, after writing *Europe's Next Powerhouse? The Evolution of Chelsea Under Emma Hayes*, I thought I'd temporarily retire from books and focus on my analysis and podcasting work instead. That took its toll on me but just three months after submitting the manuscript, I started to get the itch again. It was only in March 2022 that I thought of realising the vision of a book on the England women's team, and from there this journey began.

The mental focus required to home in on a topic that needs a deeper level of understanding requires you to solely concentrate on itself and block out all other distractions, especially when the deadline looms closer. But despite all of the physical and mental fatigue I went through at the end of the process, the feeling of accomplishment is like nothing else. But why international football, you may ask?

The concept of *Lionesses: Gamechangers* wasn't obvious at first but the more I thought about it, the more it made sense. I've been following the Women's Super League and Women's Champions League for almost four years now and my first real exposure to the women's game was the 2019 World Cup. Going back and paying homage to the football that introduced me to a different life was a fitting way to round off this set of books. Two back-to-back summer tournaments with positivity surrounding a team filled with generational stars that promised to deliver but had never yet really crossed the finish line made for the perfect storm. Moving away from writing about clubs that have distinct and dynamic tactical changes to that of an international team whose tactical identity sees only incremental changes would prove to be a new and enticing challenge.

I wanted to approach this book differently from the way I had written my earlier titles. A diverse structure and a unique way of delivering the content to a wider audience – including tacticians and fans alike – was my primary goal and I think I've delivered on that promise. A clear timeline of events split into three phases heading into the 2023 World Cup gives you a much better idea of the tactical evolution Sarina Wiegman has taken this team through. Ultimately, this is and will always be the core principle of my books.

To write with as much authenticity as possible, I happened to take a trip to London to watch the latter stages of the 2022 Euros and was blessed to end up watching five games – including the exhilarating final at Wembley. The trip was a once-in-a-lifetime opportunity, not only because of the matches and their ultimate outcome, but because of the people I finally got a chance to meet. Meeting all the connections I had made over 'Football Twitter' multiple times over was incredible. Taking in the atmosphere and understanding the passion in person gave me a whole new perspective on the game. But before we start diving into the narrative, there are a few people to mention without whom this book would not be possible.

I can't start this series of thank-yous without mentioning my friend and editor Ravshan Ergashev. He's now edited all three of my books and given me feedback at will for months, checking every chapter multiple times. He made sure this book stayed on course with the new approach and had a major assist all the way through the creative process. Thank you, my friend.

My parents and sister have been very supportive of my journey, and I can't thank them enough to let me finish this book uninterrupted. It's been stressful under the shorter turnaround but I'm grateful all the same.

Abhishek Sharma makes his second appearance in the series, but he's been no less brilliant since our first encounter in 2019. His tremendous help with the visualisations makes this book that much better. Thank you, buddy, it's always a pleasure.

Domagoj and Om are two highly esteemed friends of my inner circle and ones I wouldn't have met if I never stepped into football. Their constant presence in giving me constructive feedback on my work has been a big reason for my improvement and I can't be more grateful. More than just being great analysts, they're great people as well. I had the pleasure of meeting Domagoj and his wonderful girlfriend Željka in Sheffield after watching the England v Sweden game together, and as for Om, thanks for putting up with me during our stay together!

Sophie Lawson was as much a surprise as not. She's now a full-time journalist writing over at ESPN, but you have to know that this accomplishment comes after years and years of hard work. A couple of meetings with Sophie ended up in hours of discussion over the odd tactics of the French and Dutch national teams while sipping a pink lemonade in Soho. I still want Selma Bacha at left-back and Clara Mateo as the number ten! It was a real honour to meet you, Sophie.

A special mention goes to someone I consider one of the greats of the game, and someone I consider now a friend and mentor – Willie Kirk. Willie has been extremely kind and forward with his insight, contacts, and willingness to share knowledge with me, for which I am eternally grateful. Watching France v Germany together was a major highlight of my summer.

Mia Eriksson – thank you for being a solid, supporting rock who indulged in my every moment of contentment and doubt. We share a lot of things in common and I truly thank you for talking football and life with me. You're going to do even greater things, my friend.

More thank yous to Ameé Ruszkai, Kieran Doyle, Jessy Parker-Humphreys, Rob Pratley, and Alina Ruprecht for their invaluable contributions and insights into the Lionesses, as well as the London Is Blue crew (Nick, Brandon, and Dan) for giving me the space and time to deliver this.

I've met a fair few people in the football space, but few have been as supportive and passionate as Charlene. She's been another motivational friend in the space and has a very blunt attitude to football which I respect and appreciate. Thank you, my friend.

Lastly, I need to give a huge thanks to Charlotte Stacey who wrote my foreword and someone I consider part of the inner circle. She's the founder of the On Her Side platform, an independent online magazine dedicated to celebrating professional women's football in England. Charlotte has got a real love for the Lionesses and I couldn't think of anyone better to elaborate and depict what the team means to her and her people. I hope I do your words justice.

My last book talked about not knowing my football destination, and I've still yet to figure it out. However the journey continues with its ups and downs and whether I end up in football or not is irrelevant at this point, because regardless of the outcome, I've had a hell of a time in the last four years. What happens next is what's supposed to happen. With that said, I hope you enjoy reading this as much as I enjoyed writing it.

Abdullah Abdullah

Chapter 1

The ups and downs of Phil Neville's Lionesses

NOT SINCE the days of the Mark Sampson era have the Lionesses been a competitive and coherent force, both on and off the pitch. While that regime was marred by controversy towards the end, there was no doubt that their performances under Sampson left them near the top of the rankings, fulfilling a lot of their potential.

The swift appointment of Phil Neville that followed brought about varied results to the team. While he raised the profile of the team through his well-known career at Manchester United and Everton in the eyes of the world, and continued taking the team to the latter stages of international tournaments, his tenure was ultimately less than satisfactory with a series of poor results and some dubious decisions that raised more questions than answers. What this resulted in was a team left in a limbo of trying to return to their best despite having one of the most talented squads in international football.

The main lows during Neville's time were the losses to low-ranked teams and media outbursts that made him the villain in sections of the media. The most damning indictment of his tenure was the mediocre 1-0 win against Portugal in October 2019. His assessment of the game was one of positivity, yet England clearly played poorly for large chunks of the 90 minutes. If anything, that may have summed up their form at the time – slow, sluggish, and uninspiring. Neville's only consolation was that it ended a run of five games without a win. The match was also remembered for his outburst to a young journalist who had described the previous fixture, a 2-1 defeat against Brazil, as 'tepid'. His response was that of a man who took offence, stating, 'You wanted me sacked, didn't you? Yes, you did, I read it. I read it.'

Yet there were still positives to cling on to which were significant enough to show some progress. A combination of their first SheBelieves Cup win, another World Cup semi-final, and Olympic qualification all gave the nation some hope of improvement – though it does bear mentioning that it was England's third consecutive semi-final appearance. The SheBelieves Cup run was impressive with results like a 2-1 victory over Brazil, drawing 2-2 with the United States, and defeating Japan 3-0 in the final. All three opponents were of varying degrees of difficulty, but it showed England can keep up with the best in the business.

Their 2019 FIFA Women's World Cup run saw England win Group D, beating Scotland and Argentina to qualify for the knockout phase. They closed the group with a victory over Japan, then beat Cameroon and Norway – in an impressive 3-0 result – to advance to the semi-final against the United States. They lost 2-1, faltering at that stage again before losing to Sweden in the third-place play-off.

In the wake of the World Cup exit, England's form dropped and they toiled in a series of friendlies to end the year, including a 2-1 defeat to Germany at Wembley Stadium on 9 November 2019 in front of a record attendance for an England women's match at 77,768, becoming the second-biggest crowd for a women's game in England.

England's poor form continued into 2020 as they failed to defend their title at the SheBelieves Cup. Losses to both the United States and Spain made it seven defeats in 11 games – the team's worst stretch since 2003, mounting even more pressure on Neville who admitted he was personally responsible for England's 'unacceptable' form amid increased media scrutiny.

In April 2020 Neville announced his intention to see out his contract and leave at the expiry of his contract in July 2021. However, the allure of Major League Soccer was too much to resist as Neville then resigned earlier than had been planned to become the manager of newly created Inter Miami in January 2021. It was the end of an era that many of the fans had looked forward to, given the trials and tribulations under Neville.

Despite all the negatives, Neville's integrated approach and big-game experience that he derived from his playing career were perhaps his biggest strengths. His man-management was described as 'world-class' by Bev Priestman (his England assistant) at the 2019 Women's World Cup. Former Manchester City defender Lucy Bronze said his relationship-building with players, fans, and staff had helped England to 'become a better team'.

Neville's intended style of play wasn't overly intricate and was formed by his previous stints as assistants to David Moyes at Manchester United and Nuno Espírito Santo at Valencia. His philosophy and playing style were predicated essentially on a flexible tactical approach.

Using a 4-3-3 and 4-2-3-1 as the basis of his formation, Neville intended for his team to play fast, direct football, playing through the thirds. So it wasn't 'long balls over the top'; on the contrary, he wanted his side to play incisive passes from back to front. He wanted to embed his style of play within those two formations to allow for that flexibility.

Neville wanted to ensure the ball was inevitably played in a way to create one-on-one situations, which makes sense considering the various skilful players he had at his disposal. Nikita Parris, Lauren Hemp, and Beth Mead were all high-flying wingers, capable of the spectacular on the ball. Neville wanted to exploit their strengths and create good crossing positions for Ellen White or Jodie Taylor up front.

In build-up, the central defenders would be situated wide to ensure the pitch was spread, pushing the full-backs into higher positions. The defensive midfielder would be in a position to receive the ball and act as the primary passer out from midfield. The number six would have multiple options to choose from with the number ten, two wide players, and two full-backs to aim for. If the number six – Keira Walsh in most cases – was man-marked, the two centre-backs would aim to look for either full-back. Given Bronze's attacking instincts, she was often the target and, together with the right-winger, created overload and underload combinations.

The task handed to the central midfielder was to create space by driving into the ball side to again create overloads. This opened up passing lanes for the striker to receive and combine with the second central midfielder to become a faux striking pair. Overloading one side meant the opposite flank was underloaded, allowing switches of plays to again create space.

From here, the premise was to get the wide players into one-on-one positions to create clear-cut chances for the players in the box. Subsequently, the two number eights or the number ten and number eight push forward into spaces around the striker to take advantage of the crossing opportunity, as well as to create space for the far-sided central midfielder and winger to run into.

In essence, this system is predicated on theorised movements and planned patterns combined with individual expression and freedom in the final third. The attacking players are creative and embody this style of play while retaining the level of tactical discipline required to fulfil the brief. Steph Houghton spoke in an interview with BT Sport in 2019 about England's desire to focus on their strengths and impose their style of play. This was indicative in their performances at the 2019 SheBelieves Cup where they beat Japan and the United States for the trophy.

Sarina Wiegman's signature was a priority for the FA after her impressive performances with the Dutch national team at the 2017 Euros and 2019 World Cup. She reached two finals, winning one and losing out to the elite USA in the other. Her time with the Netherlands certainly raised her profile enough on a global scale to make her one of the world's most elite and sought-after tacticians.

The appointment of Wiegman was seen as a major coup given her level of tactical knowledge shown in charge of the Netherlands, and their overall progressive approach. There was genuine excitement about her appointment and whether she could conjure and create a cohesive England team capable of winning major international tournaments.

But the transition from Neville's style of play to 'Wiegman-ball' was still going to take a little bit of time to adjust to, especially given the inherent nature of international football during the club campaigns.

The first test was UEFA Women's Euro 2022, which England emphatically won. The Wiegman era has indeed begun with a sense of excitement and progressive football. The results garnered since her appointment have been impressive, and winning the Arnold Clark Cup against Germany and Spain was England's first real test under Wiegman – which they passed successfully. So, who is Sarina Wiegman and how did she perform with the Netherlands, so much so that it tempted the FA to make her Phil Neville's successor?

Chapter 2

The Sarina Wiegman era

'Total Football is in my philosophy.'

– Sarina Wiegman

PERHAPS ONE of the keys to winning an international tournament is a collective player experience coupled with constant adaptation. This is even more the case when it comes to building a long-term project, which is a much trickier task on the international stage. Suddenly England have both. What happened in previous years could possibly put their lack of silverware down to the preceding coaches, who have perhaps been too focused on a set way of playing or an over-reliance on short-term objectives. It's an aspiration for every international team to win trophies but for England, it's been long-awaited. The team needed someone invested in the women's game with a winning mentality of wanting to push and improve the team without using them as a stepping stone.

Enter Sarina Wiegman.

The FA pinpointed Wiegman as their main target early and once they won the battle for her signature, they knew they now had a winning manager in their midst. Her tenure with the Netherlands certainly raised her profile to that of the elite. The FA's plan with her was to embark on a long-term project to make England a sustainable and impactful side capable of challenging at every tournament with a plan to integrate the next generation of players. Yet the almost immediate results brought by the Dutch coach weren't expected by even the most optimistic of supporters at the start of her reign.

Wiegman has etched her name into English and Dutch folklore as the first coach in the women's game to win two successive major tournaments. Her managerial accolades came after a playing career that at the time wasn't normal for women's football. Her time as a player took her across various parts of the world, from the Netherlands to the United States, when it was actually uncommon for players to have a spell there during the 1990s and 2000s.

Wiegman's career really started to take shape with amateur club side Ter Leede in her native Netherlands, and you could see there were early signs of her managerial traits then. In an interview with Sky Sports, her former Netherlands team-mate Jeanet van der Laan talked about Wiegman's constant communication in those days, her push to play attacking football, and her technical aspects, and she especially highlighted her leadership. This is the trait that's commonly brought up by everyone who has played with or has been coached by Wiegman. It's apparent that this skill was an inherent and natural part of her being and one that perfectly suited her as a player and coach.

During her playing days with Ter Leede, Wiegman also had a full-time job alongside her budding football career. Leadership and communication are two of the key pillars of Wiegman's managerial style, an echo from her days as a PE teacher which helped her develop those abilities within football. It was as a teacher that she first earned respect in abundance from her students, who gravitated towards her because of her effective ability to reach out to them.

Wiegman's time in the US was also a success, with her team-mates and coaches left with positive impressions. Playing for the prestigious North Carolina Tar Heels in 1989, it wasn't just a chance to compete at a high level in the college system, but an opportunity to experience a higher standard of training and facilities as well.

Since then, it has become common for a lot of players from the Women's Super League to have made temporary moves to the US college scene before starting off their careers in England and elsewhere. Lucy Bronze and Alessia Russo are just two from this current generation to have benefited from playing in the United States at some point in their careers. Incidentally, the former is also an alumnus of North Carolina Tar Heels.

Back in 1989, Wiegman played with an all-star team that year with American legends, including the likes of Mia Hamm, Kristine Lilly, Carla Overbeck, and Tracy Bates. She was able to learn and syphon information from them both on and off the pitch.

Wiegman developed her skill as a player and was described as a 'quarterback' because of her range of abilities to keep the play flowing and be technically proficient. This could go a long way towards explaining why there is such an emphasis and appreciation from her for the similar players in Keira Walsh from England and Sharida Spitse from the Netherlands.

> *'She knew the game and how to read it, I would say more so than a lot of our American players just because I think you're more around the game when you're in Europe than we were back then.'*
>
> **– Kristine Lilly for Sky Sports**

Wiegman's retirement as a player was only the beginning and saw her move into what you could say was a natural transition towards coaching. Fittingly, her coaching career began with a spell with her first prominent club, Ter Leede. Wiegman's success came quickly as she led them to the title and the KNVB Cup in 2007. She went on to set records by being the first coach of ADO Den Haag's women's team after being named earlier as the first woman to coach a men's club in the Netherlands, as an assistant at Sparta Rotterdam.

These stints didn't go unnoticed and Wiegman quickly caught the eye of the KNVB. They hired her as the assistant coach for the Netherlands' women's national team as well as the coordinator of the women's under-19 team in August 2014, both under Roger Reijners and later Arjan Van der Laan. Her best result as an assistant was reaching the quarter-finals of the 2015 Women's World Cup, and the itch to coach the national team was taking hold already. After two caretaker spells in charge following the departures of Reijners and Van der Laan, Wiegman was finally given the full-time role in January 2017.

The 2017 Euros was a chance for Wiegman to announce herself to the world and start implementing her own ideas on to the team. Going into a home tournament certainly had its own pressures but

Wiegman was determined to make a statement. It turned out to be a winning combination. Just six months after her appointment, the Netherlands won their first major international women's title. Wiegman's influence and tactical nous saw the Dutch go unbeaten throughout the whole tournament, including an exhilarating 4-2 win over Denmark in the final. It was there that she was able to really exhibit her values and principles and mould the setup to her liking. It wasn't just the team that she constructed but the surroundings to create a very solid base.

One of the first moves she made was to hire a more experienced assistant in Foppe de Haan, who quickly realised Wiegman's value to the KNVB setup. They established their job roles rather swiftly which gave them both time and space to thrive and offer the team the best environment possible. Through all of this, there was one personality trait that impressed de Haan the most – the meticulous nature in which Wiegman carried out her job. Wiegman was a stickler for details and even under immense pressure, she was able to make sound decisions. None were more pressurised than that half-time break against Denmark in the 2017 final, with the match level at 2-2. The second half saw the Dutch decimate their opponents and win 4-2.

> *'She knows what she wants but she was also open and keen to hear other people's ideas.'*
>
> **– Foppe de Haan for BBC Sport**

When it comes to her tactical culture and identity, Wiegman is very much cut from the Total Football cloth. She set out to make her Netherlands side replicate and instil the Total Football philosophy given that it's a part of the unique culture that Johan Cruyff brought to the team decades earlier. Her definition of the term is dynamic, creative, and about positional rotations. It was from there that Wiegman was able to build her Netherlands side and successfully guide them to two tournament finals. It is little wonder then that Wiegman is such a conscientious tactician and wants to ensure that every angle is covered. There's an air of simplistic complexity to her philosophy, which we saw first with the Netherlands and later with England.

Wiegman's tactics were based around a 4-2-3-1/4-3-3 hybrid involving rotations of players and a focus on attacking with the wingers. There are many similarities between Wiegman's Netherlands and England sides, with a set profile of players used in certain positions. The midfield is particularly important to Wiegman given that it's there that her best ball-players are positioned – at least it was with her Netherlands side. Jackie Groenen, Sharida Spitse, and Daniëlle van de Donk were all key personnel who linked play and ensured service was given to Vivianne Miedema. Van de Donk played a hybrid number eight and number ten role akin to Fran Kirby for England. I believe that because of the higher calibre of ball-playing centre-backs available in Alex Greenwood and Leah Williamson in Wiegman's England squad, she will look to change her point of progression to the back, despite also having Keira Walsh available. However, the core principles remain identical and they show why she was extremely successful with both the Netherlands and England.

> *'[Wiegman's] communication is absolutely key. Her consistency over the last two Euros has shown the importance. The players know exactly what's expected of them both on and off the pitch so I think that's been very key. I think the England players have appreciated her straight talking, sometimes too straight, but it guarantees clarity. It's made a massive difference to the players.'*
>
> **– Willie Kirk**

Wiegman's spell as England manager has shown signs of improvement from previous Lionesses teams in terms of their structure, cohesion, and consistency. England have taken their reliance away from individuals and leant more on a core system instead. Though Wiegman has proved her acumen once again with a win at the Euros, the World Cup presents yet another opportunity for her to stake a claim as the best international manager of her generation. Beating the likes of the USA, Brazil, and more informed European sides will be even more of a test than what she's faced so far. If Wiegman can navigate through the 2022/23 season in keeping the style of play and bringing through fresh faces, then there will be a lot of hopeful optimism going into Australia and New Zealand.

Now without further ado, sit back, relax, and enjoy the emotional roller coaster that is the journey of the Lionesses.

Chapter 3

Pre-Euros tactics – build-up

THE FIRST 18 months of Sarina Wiegman's tenure before the European Championship were always going to be intriguing. After the very predictable tactics of Phil Neville – which admittedly did see England through to a World Cup semi-final – Wiegman was seen as a tactical upgrade given her status as an international tournament winner.

I think it's intriguing to see Wiegman's fingerprints across the team at this particular moment and how quickly her methods were implemented. The pre-Euros tactics were the precursor (or theory if you will) to the application during the finals. You might be starting to wonder why I'm looking first to explain the tactics of a few friendly games instead of a major tournament. If this were a deep look into a club manager, it's unlikely there would be much of an insight to their pre-season friendlies so why should this be any different? Using the Arnold Clark Cup and the three pre-tournament friendlies gave me a chance to do a deep dive into Wiegman's mind and be conscious of what she wanted to implement before going into her first real test in charge of England.

The way I wanted to structure this book was to use this chapter as a base of comparison to the Euros and pinpoint key and precise tactical nuances for us to analyse and break down to see how the team's tactics transition to their final form.

And that is the most intriguing aspect – seeing how much England would evolve from under Neville and how effective their approach would be against different types of opposition. One of the key differences between managing a club and managing a country is that there is no luxury in just buying a player for a certain role, so coaching becomes much more important in developing a style for the team.

Though England are fortunate in having a squad that houses a multitude of styles, from ball players to creative visionaries and pure goalscorers, Wiegman wanted to create a cohesive line-up that was able to compete against both low-block and high-possession teams by using a similar structure and system.

I'll break this chapter into build-up, attacking mechanisms, and pressing/defending concepts. Each one will be explained in as much detail as possible to give you a solid foundation of England's style, which leads us into interpreting some of the more distinct and contrasting tactical plans from the Euros. This chapter is being written before the 2022 Euros to give you a sense of my thoughts and feelings before a ball has even been kicked in the finals.

When we look at England's tactical structure, it's important to understand the different areas that create a coherent and otherwise collective system. The tactics can be split into three distinct phases: build-up play, middle-third transitions, and final-third patterns. All three have their unique triggers and movements that integrate players from different areas to create a seamless flow of movement.

Wiegman's overall philosophy is to play a direct and efficient yet intelligent style of football that is also adaptable. The central defenders are very important in choosing the first action out from the back, whether it be a long ball or short pass to the central or wide areas. The full-backs have a unique role while the midfield trio are the catalyst to England's defending and attacking transition patterns. Movement defines their structure and is emphasised by Wiegman's obsession with efficient ball progressors and off-ball playmakers. These two types of role have probably defined her tenure the most so far, given she wants her England side to play fast, effective, and technical football.

England's build-up structure was as much a mystery as it was effective. There were games where they played some scintillating football out from the back, while other matches seemed a bit more chaotic with no sense of a plan, but rather a haphazard choice in the heat of the moment.

Let's take it a step back and analyse the system Wiegman utilised. She favoured a 4-2-3-1 formation with the double pivot and attacking midfielder as vital components that embodied how her side was going to play. Each of the pre-tournament friendlies – against Germany, Spain, Canada, Belgium, the Netherlands, and Switzerland – saw Wiegman use 4-2-3-1 as the starting formation with a few similarities in the build-up. What was most pertinent about England was their various methods of building out from the back.

England adopted different iterations depending on the game circumstances and depending on whether opposition teams utilised a high-pressing strategy or a low-block pattern. In either scenario, the Lionesses have implemented and used two distinct build-up patterns for ball progression. First up, it's the most commonly used method of utilising the full-back.

Part of Wiegman's thinking was how best to employ England's exceptional ball-playing ability from the back given that she was in possession of two of the best ball players in European football, Millie Bright and Alex Greenwood. Steph Houghton and Lotte Wubben-Moy are serious options too, but the former was dropped from the squad due to fitness issues while Wubben-Moy is still honing her craft. Using the centre-back pairing was key in ensuring that England were able to have an effective outlet to play out of a press while retaining possession between the thirds.

The main principle is to funnel progression through the right flank to create solo attacking situations in the wide areas through a mixture of overloads and underloads. As I've explained before, overloading one side automatically forces teams to shift across, leaving the opposite flank clearer. The setup is often built with the centre-backs split wide and the full-backs high with the number six settling vertically opposite the goalkeeper as shown in ***Figure 1***. This gives England space and time to choose their options and adjust their move based on the game state.

This illustration shows how they are ideally set up when playing out from the back. The two central defenders want to be on either side of the goalkeeper to stretch the opposition forward as much as possible to

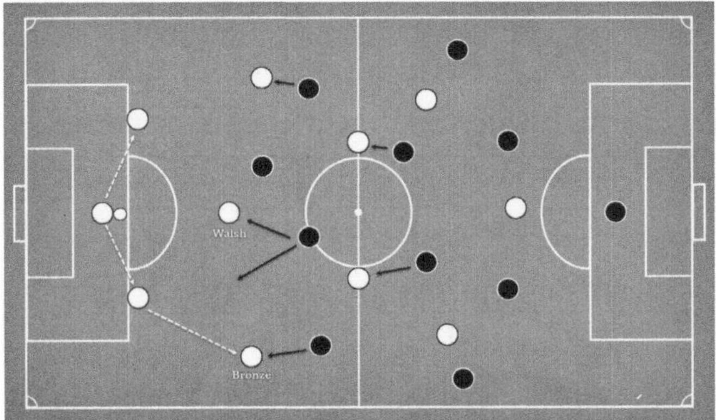

[Figure 1]

give the next pass more time. The first pass is usually towards the central defender which eventually reaches the right-back. In Lucy Bronze, England have one of the best ball progressors in world football regardless of position, and utilising her strengths in dribbling, positional awareness, and movement is critical.

The alternative is a direct pass from the goalkeeper to the right-back in the event of the keeper being pressed. The double pivot is often used when teams sit back and give Keira Walsh time and space to receive and turn, and though she's excellent under pressure, passing it to the number six against a high-pressing side can be perilous. The black arrows indicate the players who will want to press the England players in the build-up but the innate press resistance in Walsh helps to negate this to an extent.

Once the ball moves to the right-back, she'll push up and create combination plays with the ball-sided central midfielder and right-winger to create an underlapping run. This essentially creates space on the far side while also ensuring there is a passing option on the ball side. Williamson will hover around the play to give England a wall pass option and continue the link forward. The two sixes create a pendulum that works in sync with their positioning. When one pushes forward, the other holds their position and it's usually Walsh who is sitting deeper than Leah Williamson.

This build-up structure ensures the ball is played through some of England's best players to generate effective progression through the thirds. Bright, Bronze, Beth Mead, and Williamson are all involved in such a sequence of play with a combination of wall passes and short, punchy passes through midfield. Bronze is an inverted full-back which means she can drive into the interior channels and underlap while providing an extra body in midfield. This gives the right-winger space to operate and given the profiles of these players being able to thrive in one-on-one battles, it makes the final-third progression much more effective.

You might be asking, 'What about Keira Walsh and Leah Williamson being used from the outset?' You would be right in wondering why they aren't used more – but it's because most competent, high-pressing teams can single out Walsh by man-marking her, just as Alexia Putellas did when Spain played England in the Arnold Clark Cup. In staying tight to her, Putellas effectively killed any opportunity for England to use their most competent ball carrier and so resorted to the aforementioned methods of build-up. If Williamson does decide to drop deeper next to Walsh, England are outnumbered further forward if the ball does get played longer.

Alternatively, England have opted for a more direct approach – and I don't mean 'route one' football (yet); rather they want to get the ball from back to front using the quickest possible approach. The Lionesses amass a healthy percentage of possession in most games they play unless they are up against the very top sides. In doing so, they might encounter situations where teams will sit off them slightly, allowing the central defenders some space and time to operate but will nonetheless cover the central third, not allowing progression through the midfielders or full-backs as shown in ***Figure 2***. This means England need to find another way forward without giving away possession cheaply.

Wiegman wanted to do this without losing the effect of her central defenders and so she devised a plan to have Greenwood play accurate passes straight

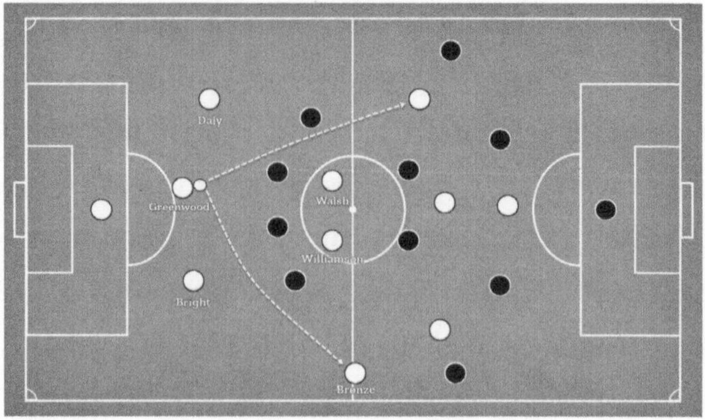

[Figure 2]

into Lauren Hemp through the channels. This sort of pass occurs with Greenwood stepping forward from the left centre-back position and threading a ball right through the channels if the opportunity presents itself. Greenwood is England's best distributor and creating situations that get her on the ball as much as possible means they can pinpoint short or long passes from the back.

Figure 3 shows how Greenwood would position herself to capitalise on this sort of scenario. Hemp would drop into the space in between the lines to create the angle for Greenwood before turning and driving forward. The strength and speed of Hemp means she can start lower and push forward if needed given how good she is in one-on-one duels.

However, ideal situations are far from realistic in most cases. In reality, teams routinely look to position

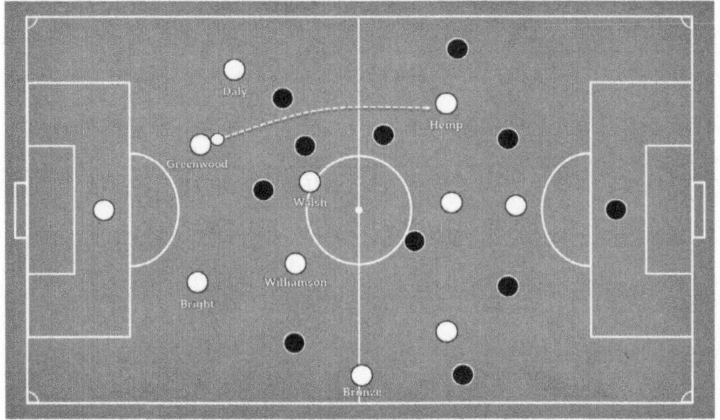

[Figure 3]

and press high up the pitch. This hurries central defenders into making quicker decisions and playing a misplaced pass or forcing the ball long where the opposition can retain possession. Of all England's principles in practice, the build-up is their greatest area of concern.

So far, they are yet to find a suitable way to play out of high-pressing situations without resorting to long, direct balls into midfield. This method of build-up goes against the 'moral values' of every top side in football, yet it is a formula that has worked for England when their first-choice options are unavailable. For them to transform and move to the next level, it will require an ethos shift of constantly trying to play out from the back where they'll make more mistakes than not. Wiegman has the players to execute this style, but they just need to 'trust the process' as they say.

If you analyse Spain and Sweden, you start to understand how repetition and confidence can change the team's outlook. In each of the friendlies, Spain, Germany, and the Netherlands had all figured out how to disrupt England's build-up through varying techniques from high-pressing to mid-blocks, thus stopping certain passing lanes into key players.

Take the game against Germany in the Arnold Clark Cup in 2022. The Germans opted for a high 4-2-3-1 out-of-possession structure to cover the passing lanes and not allow England easy channels to pass into. As such, England's usual setup was nullified by Germany using their inside-forward and striker to sit in the cover shadow of England's centre-backs while the two central midfielders would push in the space where England's midfielders would be.

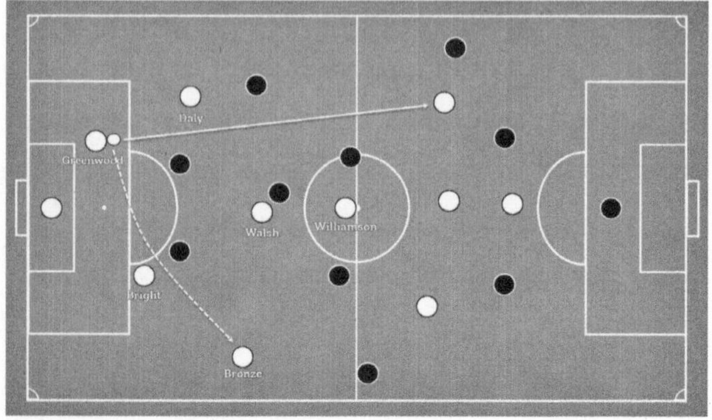

[Figure 4]

Walsh was isolated in this square and became a difficult passing option. With the full-backs high and wide, Greenwood's only other option was to go long. The depiction of this build-up sequence is shown in ***Figure 4*** where the resulting long ball is won by Germany, but immediately lands at Bronze's feet and England's build-up continues.

Spain had a similar concept but instead used two players to cover-shadow the centre-backs and goalkeeper. This time, Georgia Stanway is isolated with only her partner (not in frame) to help. This forced Hannah Hampton to go long into Jordan Nobbs, who lays a pass off to Jill Scott. The Manchester City midfielder is then immediately pressed by Mapi León and the move breaks down.

Despite all of this, we can see how England's mindset has changed from Phil Neville's time in charge. Walsh is arguably England's most comfortable ball carrier and in some ways is reminiscent of a player brought up in the Spanish school of football with the way she moves and uses the ball. Having her at the base of midfield goes a long way in dictating how England should be playing from the back. How they adjusted and improved their build-up technique for the Euros would be critical.

Chapter 3.1

Pre-Euros tactics – attacking mechanisms

IF THERE'S any part of England's tactics that seems to be the most concrete, it is their attacking strategy. Sarina Wiegman has devised a plan to get the best out of her talented attackers while trying to fit them all into a single team. Historically, the Lionesses have been blessed with world-class attacking units but at times it's been a tough job trying to get them all to work in sync at a major tournament. There are players who have been extremely effective yet there are still divided opinions among fans and the media about who should be starting.

Take Ellen White, for example. She's a player who doesn't seem to have always fitted into the last couple of managers' styles of play as she isn't best suited to their brands of football, yet she has delivered at every major tournament she's played in. A player who knows how to find the back of the net becomes extremely important. The collective structure built by Wiegman is another attempt to pull every part of the pitch together, but this could be the best approach yet.

This is probably England's most cohesive phase of play and the area of the pitch with the most depth. England's attacking plans have been a lot more dynamic, and they seem to have unleashed the potential of some of their best players. The attacking talent in Wiegman's squad is extensive with a good mixture of strikers, wingers, and attacking midfielders, with each position filled with various profiles of players of varying skillsets.

The way in which Wiegman wants her team to attack is very much in line with the strengths of the players she has at her disposal. The way England build up puts them in a good position to have their forward players in decent attacking positions.

There are two distinct sequences when it comes to forward movement patterns: how the team operates in the wide areas and the role of the number ten. These players work in tandem yet also have individual responsibilities. Both sets of players involved have a mixture of set instructions and creative freedom.

The basic principle is to create numerical advantages in the forward areas while overloading one side of the pitch to create an underload on the opposite flank. The 4-2-3-1 setup interchanges with a 4-3-3 with the second number eight pushing up to act as a number ten in the attacking phase of possession. I'll come to the role of the central midfielders momentarily, but it's their versatility in the attacking and defensive phases of play that becomes important in helping England maintain a balance and controls the transition both on and off the ball. The resulting verdict is in fact to give Lauren Hemp space to drive against her full-back and utilise her strength in taking on players in one-on-one duels.

The forwards combined are a mobile unit but each comes into their own at a particular time and place. There is heavy importance given to the wide players as Wiegman wants them to be central to the

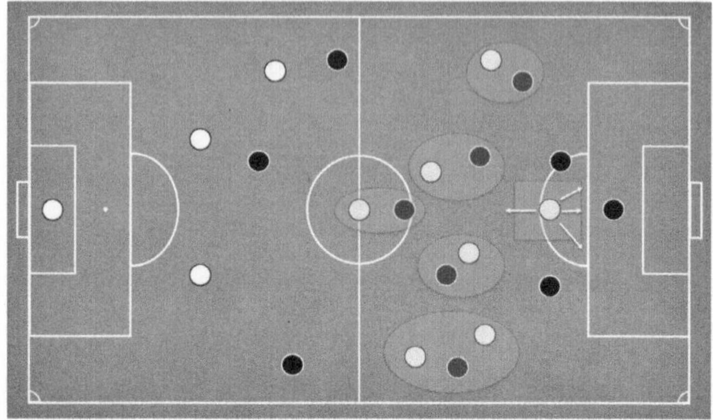

[Figure 5]

way England attack. The wingers need to be durable and interchangeable while the central striker needs to occupy the penalty area with some importance given to link up play in a vertical line rather than ghosting through to the channels.

The concept at its most basic level is illustrated in ***Figure 5*** to highlight how Wiegman wants her team to set up in most attacks. What you see here are several numerical superiorities that force teams to commit players to shift across. The central highlighted area is the sort of position that the centre-forward will occupy and manoeuvre within. The first phase is all centred around getting the ball into dangerous areas through interchanging and creating short passing triangles with the players closest to them – often the full-back, winger, attacking midfielder, and at times, the central midfielder. Wiegman wants her striker to stay central to attack the box rather than run the channels constantly. With numerous players occupying the half-space, the centre-forward needs to be ready in the middle to capitalise on the inevitable crosses or threaded balls.

The second phase is triggered when the play progresses to the point of creating the final movement or pass. What I mean by this is when England look to get the wingers/full-backs into a crossing or final passing position. I've touched upon the need for the centre-forward to stay central so that when the ball is crossed in, there are a couple of players to attack it in the box. That one-on-one moment or overlapping/underlapping movement is a sign that England are in a position to create a clear-cut opportunity.

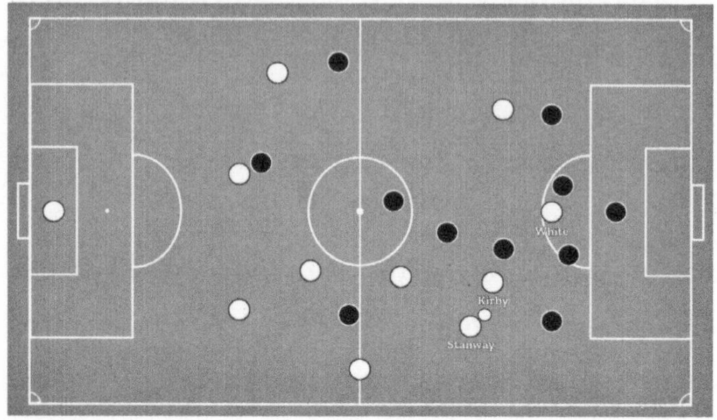

[Figure 6]

Going back to the Arnold Clark Cup, White's goal against Germany was a classic example of how England's attackers – especially the centre-forward – position themselves. In ***Figure 6***, you see a re-creation of the goal where possession starts deep with Keira Walsh with the ball played into Leah Williamson before coming inside towards Georgia Stanway. The interior movement from Fran Kirby initiates the pass towards her. While Fabienne Dongus is attracted to Stanway, Kirby is able to drive into the space, receive the pass and play it forward, and it's at this point the second phase is triggered and play speeds up. Though Kirby is lucky the ball hits the defenders and bounces back, she then passes to White, who in this entire sequence has maintained her position centrally in an area that spans the frame of the goal. Short, subtle movements enabled her to take a good first touch and score.

This is possibly why White is such a significant fit, where she's able to carry out *some* form of link-up play while ensuring she maximises her real estate space. White is a decent striker with her back to goal and using her physicality to be a connector for some of the intricate play is important. A player like Bethany England is much more suited to interchanging positions because of the tactics Chelsea use, but here she is another useful option when it comes to occupying the central space and getting on the end of high crosses.

Part of me thinks that Wiegman's use of a White-type forward is because of White herself. The role calls for a more link-up forward who can interact with the diminutive playmakers and show silky touches in build-up before taking up a central position to finish, which is why I think there are two more capable forwards to carry this out.

The first is Alessia Russo, England's other centre-forward, with a combination of skills from both

Bethany England and White. The Manchester United striker is a physical presence and a mobile player who has good movement and can connect with the players around her. If the friendly against Switzerland was anything to go by, then maybe Russo is England's eventual heir to the striker throne. There was an argument to be made that she should have been England's starting striker against Austria.

However, in my opinion, the player most suited to the role is Rachel Daly, but she is currently considered a pure full-back. Daly arguably has the best link-up and movement combination of all the forwards available. Playing as a striker for Houston Dash, Daly understands the patterns required in a mobile centre-forward and has shown traces of her intelligence when playing as a full-back. The way England play in the forward line suits Daly's game in matching her ability to occupy the box, her excellent ball control, and her spatial awareness, which allows her to be in the right positions.

Her instincts and movement patterns align with the principles of Wiegman's tactical philosophy, yet she's used primarily as a left-back. There are legitimate reasons for this, some of which I think make a lot of sense given the style of play employed, but I will be dissecting Daly and the full-backs later in the book as well as a section on England's forwards' compatibility in the side. Why Daly is such a good fit for the centre-forward position is because of how she can link up with the number ten.

The attacking midfielder is Wiegman's conduit. This player is the fulcrum that connects the defensive and attacking transitions, ensuring England constantly maintain useful possession. They're tasked with creating chances and linking play, but also in taking up goalscoring positions in and around the box. Their off-ball responsibilities are as important to the game plan.

The number ten patrols the space between the two half-spaces to support any attacks down those flanks, whether it's combination plays on the right or stretching play down the left. Their importance should not be understated. How this comes together is where the secret of playing to everyone's strength lies.

Moving on to the other attackers, the two wingers are slightly opposite profiles to each other. One is an inside-forward capable of playing in the interior channels, cutting inside and driving past players to shoot while also operating on the outside, sliding in crosses. The other winger is more of an orthodox wide forward who enjoys hugging the touchline and putting in an immense cross.

Having said that, there are hardly any wingers in the purely traditional mould now. Most of them have elements of this multi-functional, modern wide player comfortable playing both in the exterior and interior channels.

England's main focal points are the wingers. The goal is to get the ball to them and allow them space to attack the box and their opposing defender. From the right, the winger can play in small, tight spaces, using the full-back, attacking midfielder, and a central midfielder to bounce passes, and create quick combination plays when England are in possession and building up to attack. From here, the ball is either played out to the overlapping player or the winger is played through in a position to cross or shoot from the edge of the box.

On the left, the winger is usually isolated given how the focus and orientation of both teams is towards the right. In this case they stay alert and slightly inwards to receive the switch of play before bursting towards the box to cross or shoot. The left-winger is a competent one-on-one artist and is comfortable playing on both sides, though they must make split-second decisions to beat their marker. Hemp is the starting left-winger and is their best player in this position. Her ability to beat a full-back, especially when given space and room to attack, has this breathtaking quality about her when she gets on the ball that you fully expect her to whip a sublime cross in.

Creating that imbalance in the pendulum of the 4-2-3-1 requires the left-back to be much more disciplined to give the attacking player more freedom. There are times when play is routed through the left-hand side and the number ten comes across to interchange play but the aforementioned build-up and attacking strategy is still their main go-to.

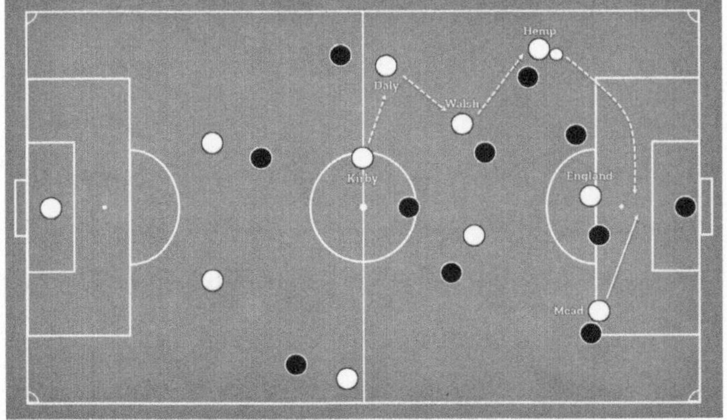

[Figure 7]

Figure 7 is what I would consider England's perfect goal. From planning to execution, the move was an archetype of a Wiegman goal. This came in the friendly against the Netherlands to make it 2-1 and was scored by Beth Mead. Though it came down the left, the principles were clearly in effect. Kirby dropped deep to connect and progress the ball, which was quickly laid off to Daly before a first-time pass to Walsh. Kirby's movement pulled two Dutch markers away and opened up the space in behind for Walsh to receive in space as she stepped off her own marker. What followed was one threaded pass between the centre-back and full-back for Hemp to run on to and cross into Mead's path in the box.

The result was essentially a diving tap-in but Mead's goal was a culmination of 18 months of work and the attacking players being settled in their roles. One of the key indicators of a settled attacking unit in this system is the ability of their rotation players to slot in and maintain the same level of performance left by the starters. The full-back roles are key to allowing the wingers to operate, as I mentioned with Hemp and the left-back. The right-back has an equally important job in playing an aggressive attacking game but has to be switched on to track back and defend the vacant space.

The central midfielder's role in the attacking mechanisms is more evident off the ball than on it. The players in the double pivot are distinctly contrasting in how they operate. The defensive midfielder sits deeper and is more of the distributor and defensive anchor – typically Keira Walsh – while the number eight is a roaming playmaker though not in its traditional definition. The premise is for this player to move between the lines and act like another number ten when England are in possession yet provides a balance in defensive transitions. The movements forward create a more 4-3-3 shape and this player is given license to attack down the right channel to help with the overloads in that area.

Leah Williamson has been Wiegman's preferred central midfielder given her composure and presence defensively, but also in an attacking capacity. Using Williamson in this role is a clear sign of balance for the 'big' games where England can move their tactics from possession-based to a counterattacking style and vice versa. Both Walsh and Williamson provide that. What we saw against the Netherlands, Germany, and Spain was a tactical battle that needed this sort of double pivot. Williamson drove into the half-spaces not only to receive but also to create more space for the right-winger and number ten to attack the spaces in behind and receive in influential pockets near the edge of the box.

The other option is to drop Williamson into her more natural centre-back role, but England are still searching for another number eight who can be more aggressive and consistent in the games in which they have much more possession and will be situated in the opposition half for most of the 90 minutes. The first half against Switzerland in their final warm-up game was an indication of this. Stanway was chosen as the central midfielder for that game and showed glimpses of a more attack-minded number eight, but her off-the-ball work needed improvement after giving away some cheap fouls. However, this is the sort of role England want from the central duo.

Off-the-ball work is another important aspect of the way England attack. As another method of creating chances, the Lionesses employ a man-marking system that uses a mid-block shape and presses again in a 4-2-3-1 or 4-2-4 shape. They do press aggressively, but a lot of that comes from different triggers – mainly in counterpressing situations. Winning the ball back becomes important and if they do manage to gain possession high up the pitch, it becomes easier for the fluid forwards to capitalise. But given how a lot of their duels are engaged centrally, the double pivot steps in to trigger their defensive duties and apply pressure. ***Figure 8*** shows England's duel map, against the Netherlands and Germany, displaying where they won back the ball.

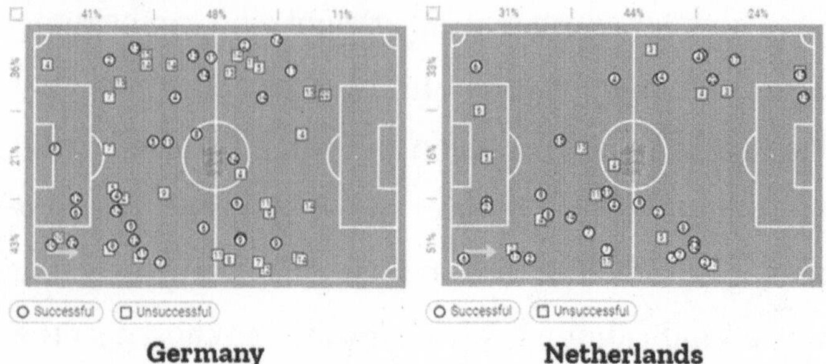

[Figure 8]

The pressing shape becomes important and there will be a more in-depth explanation of this in the next chapter, so it's good to get a sound idea of how else the forwards create chances. This demands and breeds a high work rate, and a willingness to win the ball back and exploit the unorganised back lines.

Wiegman has instilled a belief in and revitalised a few players in this squad, like Beth Mead, who now looks to be a mainstay. I think her memo would have highlighted the imperative to get her forwards firing on all cylinders consistently as a priority, but being able to ensure the benched players come on and slot in seamlessly has Wiegman going above and beyond what is expected in a relatively short amount of time, given how long international managers have with their squads.

England were starting games slowly but if these friendlies were anything to go by, then it shows the level they were at before the tournament.

Now, let's look at what key nuances came out of the 2022 European Championship.

Chapter 3.2

Pre-Euros tactics – pressing and defending

WE NOW arrive at the part of the book where England were, and currently are, probably the most stocked in terms of depth. This is where the real test lies in going through a major international tournament and repelling top sides. Their back four is one of the most effective both individually and collectively.

Perhaps it is the nature of the personnel at hand, or just the inherent expectation that comes with England, but defending and pressing looks to be an area they are most secure in.

Sarina Wiegman's defensive unit has mainly come up against minnows but facing the likes of Germany, Spain, the Netherlands, and Switzerland gave us a good idea of where they stood. Clean sheets against the latter three and one goal conceded against Germany meant my claim on England's capacity to defend against the very best is validated.

So far so good for the Lionesses and going into a home tournament off the back of some impressive defensive performances always bodes well for their chances of winning. Indeed, it is a side's defensive qualities that are the foundation of a winning team. José Mourinho's Inter Milan or Thomas Tuchel's Chelsea side were classic examples of how diligent defending was the catalyst to their Champions League exploits. Wiegman's own Dutch side of 2017 was built upon creating a hard-to-beat mentality leveraging their stellar front line. She is attempting to do the same with England with arguably better defenders.

How she wants to defend is reflective of the way England are looking to set up their attacking patterns and give themselves a solid structure to transition effectively. Using both trigger-based pressing patterns and compact defensive shapes, Wiegman is connecting a collective defensive power and individual strengths in defence together. The central defenders are strong individually while the full-backs are very quick and sound positionally. The screens in front of the back four have distinct roles off the ball and are able to switch between their attacking and defensive duties. However, England's defensive work starts from the front where they use a pressing style that attempts to force high turnovers for England to counterattack.

England's in-possession and out-of-possession shapes are similar but can diverge from time to time. In their build-up games they operated with a 4-2-3-1 and 4-4-2 defensive shape, depending on where the opposition were on the pitch. England often look to press from the front and will situate themselves in a 4-2-3-1 shape, trying to block off passing lanes and give themselves a man-to-man marking style to engage and press. When the opposition are in the middle third or further ahead, England will prioritise and move into a 4-4-2 shape and ensure the central spaces are blocked off before engaging in duels.

Their pressing is staggered and is based on triggers but is most pertinent once the ball is played out from the back. However, this isn't to say they are completely averse to a high-pressing structure – on the contrary, England will frequently press high up the pitch depending on the opposition at hand. Take Spain for instance, a team that utilises a very possession-intensive system and will almost always play out from the back. However good they are on the ball, they do have a tendency to relinquish possession under the right amount of pressure.

A lot of the time we'll see this high press in counter-pressing sequences when the Lionesses lose the ball and want to retain it quickly against teams that have a weakness in defensive transitions, and these pressing zones are usually found in the middle third where they have committed the defending team forward enough.

All of this can be packed into three core principles: 1) compactness; 2) blocking central access; 3) quick turnovers.

When operating in the 4-2-3-1 defending shape, the centre-forward and two wingers will be positioned slightly narrower and allow the centre-backs to pass between themselves and the goalkeeper. The attacking midfielder is tasked with cover-shadowing the number six so that they cover all obvious passing lanes. They're tasked with pressuring the left and right central defenders when they decide to step forward and attempt to play through the middle. England want the ball to be played into the wide areas to create a pressing trap. The attackers will angle their runs to force the centre-backs to pass in that direction, as shown in ***Figure 9***.

The only free player(s) are the centre-backs, who have the freedom to play a pass forward, but that pass becomes difficult to choose. As you can see, each

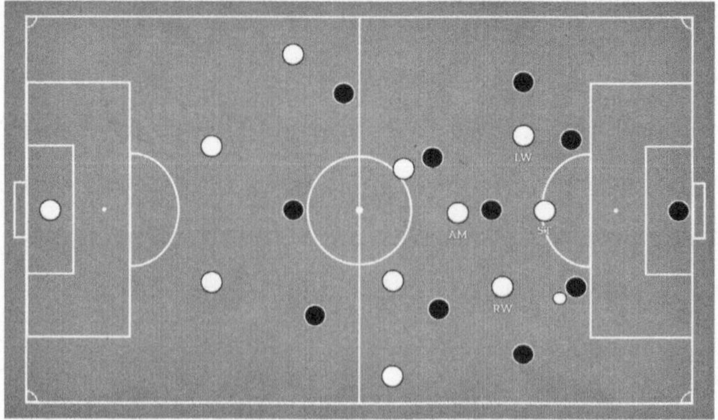

[Figure 9]

player in the illustration ensures there are no easy passing lanes.

The next defensive phase occurs once the ball reaches the opposition full-back, and this becomes a trigger for the ball-side winger and full-back to start pressing the new ball carrier. The central midfielder hovers around the half-space to protect the interior passing lane, once again forcing the ball carrier to play down the line. This pressure creates mistakes and England can counterattack from here.

Once the ball is played to the opposition left-back, the right-winger and right-back both step forward to press and close the space. In the event the left-back chooses to play a pass inside, the central midfielder will step forward and apply pressure.

A clear example of this can be taken from the England vs Netherlands game where in the illustrated

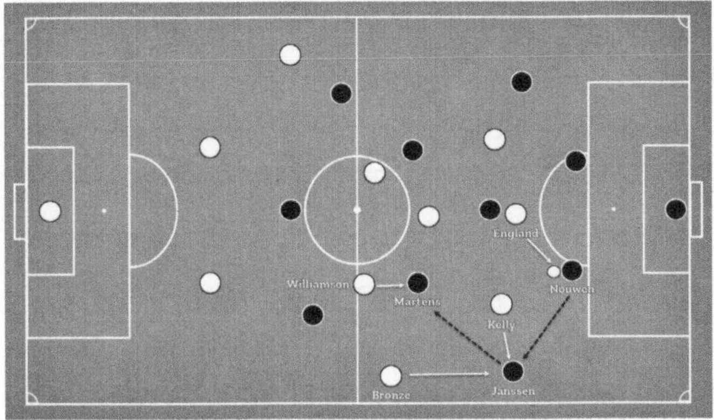

[Figure 10]

scenario in ***Figure 10***, striker Bethany England closes down Dutch centre-back Aniek Nouwen, leaving her the sole option of playing the ball out to Dominique Janssen. This pass prompted Chloe Kelly to press Janssen with Bronze in close support. The Dutch left-back instead chose to pass inwards to Lieke Martens though Leah Williamson was in close vicinity. Despite Martens getting the turn, Williamson was able to then dispossess the winger and initiate an England counterattack.

The pivot players have a critical role in how England defend in the middle third of the pitch. The forwards will press but require the central midfielder(s) to step forward and cover any spaces in behind, and this is where Williamson becomes such an important player in this number eight role. In tandem, both midfielders will look to cover their horizontal space and each other when they push forward. You'll hardly ever see both midfielders pushing up together, as the tactical discipline to be positionally aware comes from the intelligence both Walsh and Williamson possess. If you refer back to the previous chapter and review ***Figure 8***, you'll notice that 48 per cent of England's defensive duels occurred in the middle third against Germany, backing this notion of a triggered press.

There are different combinations of midfield pivots that can be used, but the box-to-box and deep-lying playmaker pairing seems the most balanced option across most games. Usually, you'll see a sole defensive midfielder burdened with the responsibility of covering and distributing but England share those duties between two players. Patricia Guijarro (Spain) and Fabienne Dongus (Germany) are two examples of players who dictate their team's attacking and defending transitions.

The number of times Walsh and Williamson appear in pressing zones at every opportunity in their vicinity is impressive, but what is more interesting is the speed at which they transition play and create a switch. Walsh's diagonal crossfield passes give England a huge advantage in counterattacking turnovers.

This transitions us nicely into rest defence. The concept is about how good a team's defensive positioning is before possession is lost to prepare for a turnover. How a team is able to cope with the transition is determined by how they're set up without the ball. Rest defences are about having numerical advantages behind the ball.

England's attacking system sees them use a 3-2 or 3-1 defensive structure depending on how far forward the ball is. This isn't ideal if they're coming up against teams that transition and play with three or four players going forward. Given that one central midfielder is playing higher up the pitch, it can be said that their defensive transition structure needs better protection, especially when the Lionesses' right-back pushes forward and leaves space in behind.

This then makes the choice of attacking midfielder a significant one given how they are partly responsible for the first phase of pressing and will need to help as a supporting body. England possess various profiles in this position with each one utilised for different game states. However, the ideal player is one that is mobile, can man-mark, press, and also play between the lines with exquisite positional awareness to block off passing lanes, as well as provide cover for the players in the first line of the press (i.e. the wingers and the striker).

As we can see in ***Figure 11***, the number ten needs to protect the highlighted areas to ensure there are

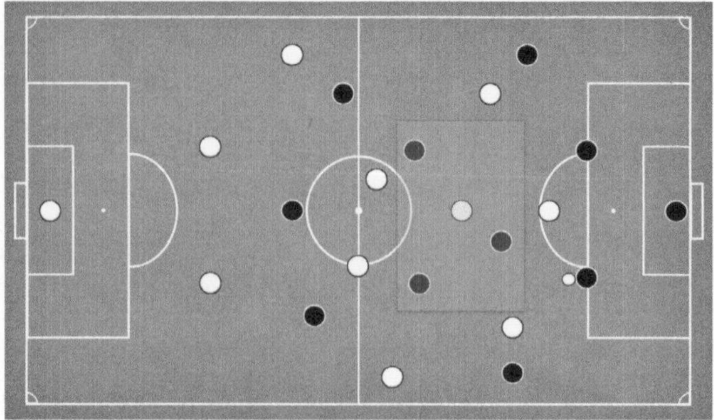

[Figure 11]

no easy routes centrally and provide extra pressing support when the ball makes its way to the wide areas. A lot of the time, the by-product of this mid-to-high press is the opposition will opt to play long rather than out from the back, which gives England an advantage in winning the aerial duels. Lucy Bronze, Leah Williamson, Millie Bright, and Rachel Daly are all excellent aerial duellists.

In a 4-4-2, England's core principles do not change. Defensive compactness and central access are still key to their approach with the main aim to make it hard for the opposition to find goalscoring chances. There are some similarities to the way Olympique Lyonnais executed their defensive structure during the 2021/22 season, using two rotating central midfielders to help cover-shadow and not afford extra space which in turn creates an over-reliance on the opposing wingers and full-backs. Using a measured man-marking system with certain triggers can create counterattacking transitions to exploit given the pace out wide. However, there are still a couple of issues for them to be wary about.

Any team that decides to play in front of England's defence makes it easier for the Lionesses to defend because of the way they shape up in a 4-4-2 or 4-2-3-1. They become much more exposed and threatened once runners make runs in behind, just as Klara Bühl did behind the full-backs for Germany versus England in February 2022. The German's runs in behind were a result of the England full-backs being caught high where their rest defence wasn't properly structured and was not sufficient for the counterattacking game that Germany played.

It is well documented that England's full-backs are encouraged to drive forward, especially from right-back. This player is the catalyst in the build-up, and she orchestrates the movements and choices players in the right space make. In doing so, England have excellent presence and overloads, but there is one prevailing issue of the pay-off which is the space left in behind. Any time there's a turnover, England are left exposed in those spaces and while the right-back is fit enough to track back, the shift across from the defenders means

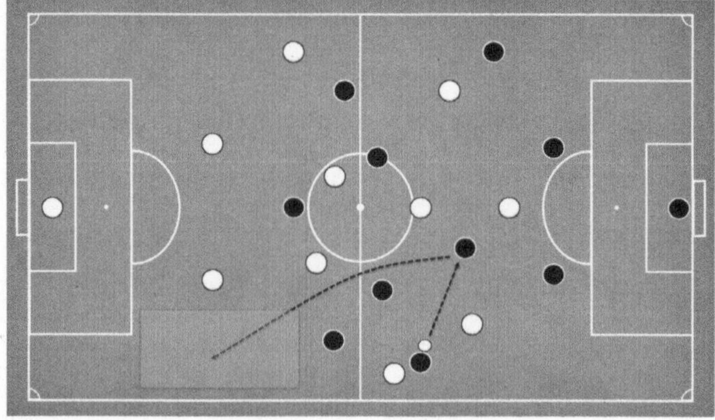

[Figure 12]

there is a chance for teams to penetrate and exploit, which can be seen in ***Figure 12***.

The highlighted area is often where teams will leave the most space. Teams are accustomed to allowing the wide areas to be free in order to give themselves time to organise; however, in a counterattacking scenario, this isn't ideal. While Bronze is still a world-class right-back and one of England's fittest players, she isn't the player she once was with her pace waning over time. Extra protection and adjustments need to be made to compensate for her higher positioning.

Rectifying this ahead of the Euros was definitely a priority. Yes, England only conceded one goal and that too was from a set piece against Germany rather than open play, but teams will target them in this area. Their main solution was to condense the space as quickly as possible and try to delay the opposing left-winger from crossing the ball in quickly. Having Bright and the defence shift across and use Walsh as cover while Bronze and Williamson tracked back became a standard defensive transition tactic.

England's defensive output mainly relies on shape and overloads to win the ball back. They aren't a *gegenpressing* team, but they do look for counterpressing situations to use the pace they have going forward. The idea to create turnovers in vulnerable situations where the opposition has committed players forward for England to then counterattack and exploit the vacant spaces is an acceptable game plan, but one that requires stringent positional discipline. England's personal choices determine this and with more understanding of the system, this seems like a positive way forward.

Chapter 4

Euro 2022 – the introduction

THE BUILD-UP, anticipation, and excitement for the 2022 Women's Euros – which had been brewing up for 18 months – finally came to fruition when 6 July edged closer and closer. The first game of the tournament, between England and Austria, was the most-anticipated fixture of the summer, and it signalled the start of what could only be described as the perfect follow-up to an exhilarating European club season.

It was a momentous occasion for not just the sport but women's football as a whole, at its peak with star players in their prime and more teams primed to make their mark on the continental stage. Austria, Norway, Italy, Denmark, and Switzerland were all underdogs gunning to break the clique and enter the knockout stages. On the other side, you had some top teams with seemingly endless talent and a genuine case for winning the tournament, like England, Spain, France, Sweden, and Germany. Each team had their own story leading up to the event and a squad of players capable of beating the very best.

Take Sweden, the silver medallists in 2021's Olympic Games and third-place finishers at the 2019 World Cup. They were 2021's team to beat with players such as Kosovare Asllani, Fridolina Rolfö, Magdalena Eriksson, and Stina Blackstenius. Each one was a serial winner with an elite mentality. In Peter Gerhardsson Sweden had a shrewd, tactical manager who engineered a way to get everyone playing to one tune. Though expectations were high coming into the finals, they were desperate to finally achieve success.

The French are never far from controversy and yet again it marred their preparations for Euro 2022. Corinne Diacre decided to leave Amandine Henry and Eugénie Le Sommer out of the squad, causing widespread uproar across the world. Yet their options were still littered with young talent capable of beating any team on their day. In 2019, France had played a World Cup on home soil with a squad in their prime and filled with immense talent all over the pitch. It was their moment.

Alas, they were knocked out in the quarter-final stage by the United States and failed yet again to win an international tournament. Moments like these are hardly consistent and with each passing year, it becomes harder and harder to replicate given the constant and exponential growth of the women's game. France needed a win, or at least a final appearance.

Meanwhile, a lot was expected from Spain for Euro 2022, but more squad selection issues pre-tournament coupled with the injury to the talismanic figure of Alexia Putellas ultimately marred their preparations. Despite this, Spain's squad looked a class above the rest with a core group featuring players from Barcelona and Real Madrid who finally looked like they might just have figured out how to synergise the different entities together.

Jorge Vilda was the man under pressure to make it happen. Fanfare aside, his man-management and indecisiveness in having a secondary plan for creating a cohesive midfield setup with the absence of Putellas meant that faith in his methods was wearing thin from the Spanish fans. They were expected to make the latter stages of the tournament and their loss came when they performed probably at their best in the quarter-finals against England.

And lastly, Sarina Wiegman and England might have gone into the finals under arguably the most pressure of them all. A home tournament with an international-calibre manager who had won the previous iteration of the Euros with the Netherlands meant big things were expected of them. Looking at it from afar, you could analyse and see a squad that seemed literate in her school of football though they did stumble here and there as the summer drew nearer.

Wiegman's management and philosophy were drilled into the players and changes made in the way they organised themselves created a better setup. Wiegman mentioned that England were more resilient and confident after her arrival, and you could see that in the way they approached each game until the very end. Though pre-tournament England seemed to suffer from underwhelming first halves, they would eventually make good comebacks for the second. They seemed to shake off the nerves during the tournament itself and peaked just at the right moment.

We witnessed numerous plans, from minor adjustments to wholesale changes, but the most impressive part of Wiegman's approach was the impact of the substitutes. Each player completely understood the assignment and slotted in without a drop in quality. Chloe Kelly, Alessia Russo, and Ella Toone were all particularly vital in helping England lift the trophy and this collective effort ensured the perfect tournament.

This phase of the book is meant to capture, understand, and analyse the key moments of the Euros – where England excelled, stumbled, and overcame adversity. I have looked to find tactical complexities, individual performances, and Wiegman's solutions to opposition tactical adjustments. Highlighting moments from the knockout ties and the group stage, the Norway game showcases how this England side put the theory and practice into reality.

Let's start with the singular most important moment that set up the path for the Lionesses' Euro victory – the 8-0 win against the Scandinavians.

Chapter 5

Norway – how Georgia Stanway dominated in England's midfield

'Georgia Stanway was absolutely crucial to everything England did. She offered great tactical flexibility in midfield to complement Keira Walsh.'

– Willie Kirk

ENGLAND'S DRAW at the European Championship was met with excitement and some caution. Austria, Norway, and Northern Ireland made up Group A together with the hosts and while they weren't exactly the toughest competition, the fixtures gave the Lionesses a platform to slowly gain momentum against the tougher tests.

Austria are a team imprinted with a formidable and hard-to-break-down mentality, accompanied by a star-studded midfield including Laura Feiersinger,

Sarah Puntigam, and Sarah Zadrazil. England's curtain-raiser was to be against them at Old Trafford and the opening match in front of a packed crowd in a home tournament was pressure like no other. The Lionesses coped and came out 1-0 victors with a subdued performance, so needed a more convincing display for their second game.

The match against Norway became crucial, not just for the three points but that the performance had to be on par with what people had come to expect from England. Norway were the team to beat in the group and were expected to progress along with the Lionesses, especially considering the quality of names featured within the squad. Ada Hegerberg, Caroline Graham Hansen, Guro Reiten, Frida Maanum, and Maren Mjelde are just a handful of the players who have proven their quality over and over again at Europe's elite clubs, from Olympique Lyonnais to Barcelona and Chelsea. Going into the second match of the group stage, there was a quiet and nervous energy among supporters, not knowing exactly what to expect – but that was quickly put to bed after Georgia Stanway's 12th-minute penalty.

That moment created a knock-on effect leading England to completely dominate the Norwegians with a monumental landslide 8-0 win. It was a truly landmark occasion, not just for the records, but as an era-defining moment for Sarina Wiegman's side. The performance, other than the sheer number of goals, was something of a marker laid down to signal the arrival of the 'new' England. Ellen White, Lauren Hemp, and Beth Mead all starred under the lights at the Amex Stadium with a scintillating display that had swagger, suave, and class. The movement and decision-making between the three was exceptional and set up England to race to a 6-0 lead in the first half.

However, it was the deeper midfielders who provided them with the solid base to allow the forward line to operate with clear fluidity, particularly Bayern Munich's Stanway. The way she and Keira Walsh functioned meant they weren't overrun defensively yet were also able to commit numbers going forward to create channel overloads and overlaps.

The previous chapter, about England's attacking system, was designed to explain how the forward line operates and the displays in the group stage showed how far they've developed tactically under Wiegman. The seemingly last-minute change of leaving out Alex Greenwood on the eve of the tournament to use Leah Williamson as a central defender appeared strange given her success as their premier left-sided centre-back and Williamson's triumph as a defensive pivot. However, the last friendly, against Switzerland, gave the Lionesses another dimension with some elite-level progressive play from the Arsenal and England captain.

The switch of personnel and position was a more progressive move, especially in games England knew they could dominate, so while it might have seemed more routine to make this decision against Austria, against Norway it wasn't as obvious. Hegerberg, Graham Hansen, Maanum, and Ingrid Engen are all threats between the lines and having a solid foundation to deal with their movements becomes critical.

Wiegman settled on the 4-2-3-1 shape but what was prevalent was the continuous adjustments England made in the system in attacking and defending transitions. They switched between a 4-2-3-1, 4-1-4-1, and 4-3-3 in possession and opted for a 4-4-2 or 4-4-1-1 without the ball. The 4-1-4-1 was significant as it showcased England playing with dual number tens instead of two number eights. Kirby and Stanway were key components in creating havoc between the lines, making line-breaking runs and passes in tandem.

The main motive to constantly shape-shift was because of Norway's 4-4-1-1 formation and the imperious threats of Hegerberg's and Graham Hansen's ability to operate between the lines and drift between England's double pivot.

The double pivot is fundamental to the balance of any line-up and their spatial awareness and positioning are crucial to a side's fundamental core principles. Without it, teams will lack any sort of transition ability and leave wide-open spaces. This game was quite the opposite as both teams used their midfield as screens to create central blockades.

Hegerberg's movement as a dropping forward is exquisite given her well-known exploits for her club, and the combination with a fluid attacking midfielder in Graham Hansen is a deadly prospect. Williamson might have been the safer choice but using the double pivot of Stanway and Walsh ended up being a much more aggressive choice and ultimately yielded more, which enabled Kirby as well. The midfield structure was constructed with one goal in mind – to disrupt Norway's midfield pivot and create overloads in the channels that constitute one of their core game philosophies.

Norway's midfield four consisted of two central players and two wingers. Though Reiten does create numerical superiority for the flat-four structure by cutting inside in the final third, England were nonetheless able to maintain a numerical advantage through Walsh, Stanway, and Kirby.

Stanway's role was particularly intriguing, playing as a hybrid number eight dropping deep to receive in the build-up while also being an advanced number ten. While Walsh's role was mainly a deep-lying distributor that enabled England to build out and distribute both long and short, Stanway was very much the instigator and progressor. The tenacity in Stanway's game meant she was able to carry out the role while adjusting to the match state. Part of the reason for her use as a number ten was because of the tenacity she brings as well as creativity. Her off-the-ball discipline was the biggest concern but if the Austria and Norway games are anything to go by, then it's proof that Stanway can be a long-term option as a number eight, but that can be discussed later.

This example in ***Figure 13*** might be a classic example of build-up and progression but the positions

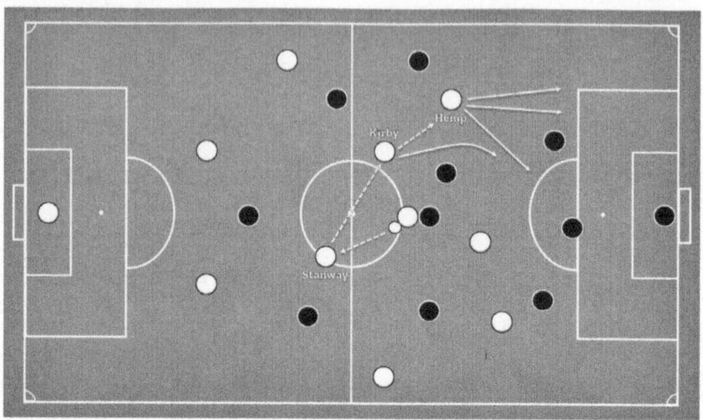

[Figure 13]

of the players remain the same. The first ball was won by Norway, but the second ball picked up by Stanway already shows how England have a numerical advantage in a three-v-two in midfield. The pass out to Kirby highlights the Chelsea playmaker in space and is able to free up Lauren Hemp on the left, who can receive the ball and subsequently pushes Kirby forward too. Equally, if the centre-forward made the run to the right, she would find herself in the same amount of space too. Stanway's deeper position showcases the versatility in her movement and positioning in that game, coming into a deeper space to protect the back four for the shorter pass before it went long.

While I've mentioned Norway's midfield line being a flat four to some extent, the interior positions taken up by Reiten meant there were times of a central block of three instead. Wiegman instructed her trio of interior midfielders to be positioned on either side of the Norwegian double pivot to take advantage of the half-space regions to receive and progress in space. At various points throughout the first half, England were able to receive in space without any real pressure of being dispossessed. Stanway pushed up while Kirby dropped deep and vice versa, with both players creating the 4-1-4-1 shape. An example of this can be partially

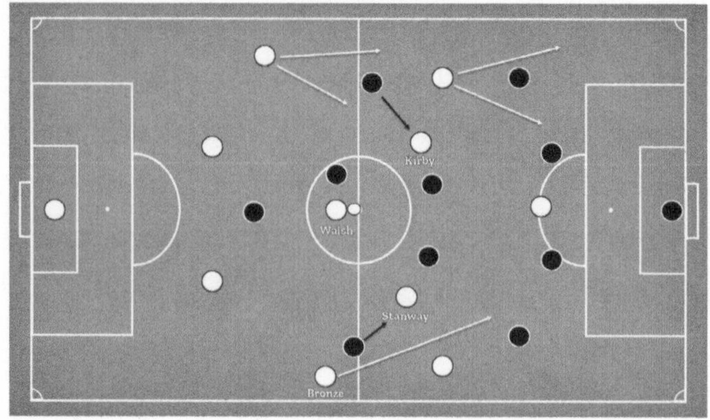

[Figure 14]

seen in the earlier example, but here is another one in ***Figure 14***.

Though this is a simple passing sequence starting with Walsh, both Kirby and Stanway are positioned in slightly wider positions – mainly Kirby – in relation to the Norwegian central midfield duo. The threat of England's wide players forces the full-backs to stay tight, thus leaving the half-spaces open for Kirby and Stanway to utilise. The apparent weakness of Maria Thorisdottir's and Maren Mjelde's defending down their sides was in turn heavily exploited by the movements of Kirby and Stanway, as well as Lucy Bronze's interior runs.

This sequence in ***Figure 15*** highlights how Stanway drifted into the wide space and ran the channel through the vacant spaces and then interchanged with Mead. The Arsenal winger held up the ball and waited

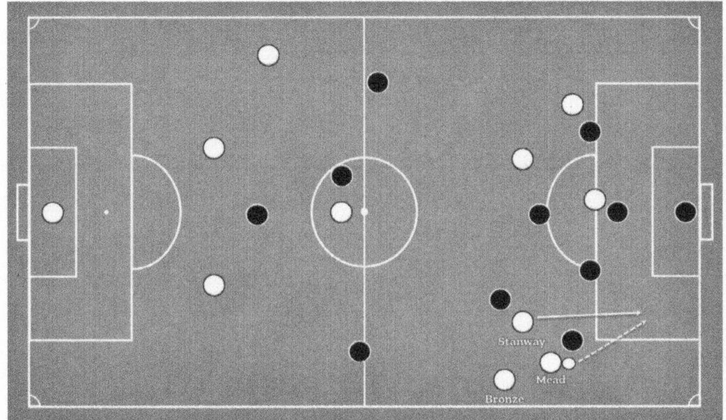

[Figure 15]

for an opportunity to play another pass. Stanway drove into the box through the Norwegian defence and found herself in acres of space to cross the ball into the box.

A lot of Norway's issues stemmed from their defensive structure mismatch with out-of-position personnel but make no mistake – England's movements would still have caused most teams a lot of issues. Going forward, this approach may still need to be optimised and adjusted against higher-level opposition. However, this game was probably a very strong representation of Wiegman's solution to their central midfield position if she wanted to persist with Williamson as the central defender.

Chapter 6

Spain – the pressing threat

THE DAY after my arrival in London saw me travel to Brighton for my first Euro game, sitting among the Spanish supporters at the Amex Stadium. The caved-in feel of the stadium created an electric atmosphere and my vantage point gave me a perfect view of England's right-sided build-up and off-the-ball work in the first half. Analysing a game live in person provides a holistic view over the isolated TV angles that limit what can be seen around the active area of play.

England's run to the quarter-final had gone pretty much as planned. Big wins against Norway and Northern Ireland set the stage for the tournament after a nervy opening victory against Austria. Until the quarter-finals, the Austrians proved to be England's toughest test given their solid, compact structure under Irene Fuhrmann.

Spain's run to this stage was, in contrast, not as smooth since they had come in with mixed results in the group stages. A 4-1 win over Finland after going 1-0 down showed resilience but a 2-0 loss to Germany was humbling. A much-needed win against Denmark meant Spain went through as runners-up in their group and faced England in the last eight.

The Spaniards, however, presented a different proposition, as Jorge Vilda's side had the tools to cause problems for England. Tactically, their style of play was structured enough to be composed yet flexible enough to keep possession and play around England efficiently. Their in-possession game is probably the most stylish on their day and their out-of-possession game is at a high level given that the Spanish players are positionally some of the best in the game, especially in midfield. Tension in Spain over Vilda's inability to bring out the best of the talented squad at his disposal was a theme pre-match.

The core of the side is made up of the Barcelona spine, though comparisons between the club side and national team are constantly played down. Mapi Léon, Irene Paredes, Patri Guijarro, Aitana Bonmatí, and Mariona Caldentey were the Barça spine of the team surrounded by talents from Real Madrid, Atlético Madrid, and Real Sociedad. When you look at the calibre of players within the Spanish setup and their collective success in Europe, you begin to understand why they were well equipped to challenge the Lionesses.

Sarina Wiegman's group had been effective in playing against compact sides but the teams they had faced so far weren't the best in progressive play. The games in the Arnold Clark Cup showed there were some weaknesses in creating openings, namely the 0-0 draw against Spain. Germany were a more transition-based team without their best defenders but even then England took time to break them down, eventually winning 3-1. There are some underrated parts to the English cog. Their midfield consists of Keira Walsh, Fran Kirby, and Georgia Stanway, who in their own right are three top players in their roles. Walsh in particular was underrated in how important she was to this England team.

Wiegman's basic possession principles remain intact until teams start finding opportunities to break through the English structure. This game was the first where England faced a stern test and were being outplayed until Ella Toone's equaliser. The first 84 minutes gave us a glimpse into how a team could break England down, particularly by denying the Lionesses their pressing sequences. There were two distinct tactical nuances that Spain applied to nullify England's progression and transition game.

The game plan

Wiegman's team had been impressive throughout the tournament, not just for their impressive performances in each match, but the pace at which they had settled into her tactical identity. The way in which she instilled her ideas into the squad in a little over 12 months is exquisite, especially against the stronger sides.

One very impressive aspect of Wiegman's philosophy is the off-the-ball work, particularly the team's pressing structure. Wiegman emphasises the need to work tirelessly off the ball and England's incessant pressing has been a highlight of her tenure so far. However, Spain nullified their press enough to bypass the front lines and enable progression through midfield. To know how they did that, let's see what England's game plan was in the first place.

England started in their usual 4-3-3 formation with the same team that started every game of the Euros. Walsh, Stanway, and Kirby made up the midfield trio while the back four of Luzy Bronze, Millie Bright, Leah Williamson, and Rachel Daly remained intact. Beth Mead, Lauren Hemp, and Ellen White were the front three. The system is constantly changing between the

4-3-3 and 4-2-3-1 and is the basis of both their on-the-ball and off-the-ball shape. At times they used a 4-4-2 off-the-ball structure here but regardless, the idea was to create compactness. They attempted to go to the 4-2-3-1 formation from goal kicks to stop build-up and had to adjust their standard style for Spain.

To recap, the England pressing structure sees Bronze pushing up while England hold a back three of sorts with Mead and the right-sided interior midfielder stepping across to create a vacuum to press. They force teams to the wide positions but almost insist on going down their right since their build-up and structural build is heavily based on the right side. Bronze and Mead are very aggressive and wanting to switch play and give Hemp space is the source of the idea here.

Spain understood England's intentions and were relying on the ball-carrying abilities of Mapi León and Irene Paredes to break up the structure. The Barcelona centre-back pair are excellent at reading the game and playing out of high presses. The Lionesses knew they would be expecting the high press and instead applied measured pressure and so allowed them space to step forward before opting to close them down.

The plan was simple: give Mapi León and Paredes time – but not too much time – and limit entry into

Patri Guijarro. The Barcelona defensive midfielder is a monster. She's got the vision, composure, and passing range of a top-class creative midfielder while being positionally exquisite. She is the heartbeat and engine of Spain and stopping her means suffocating the Spaniards as I've illustrated in ***Figure 16***.

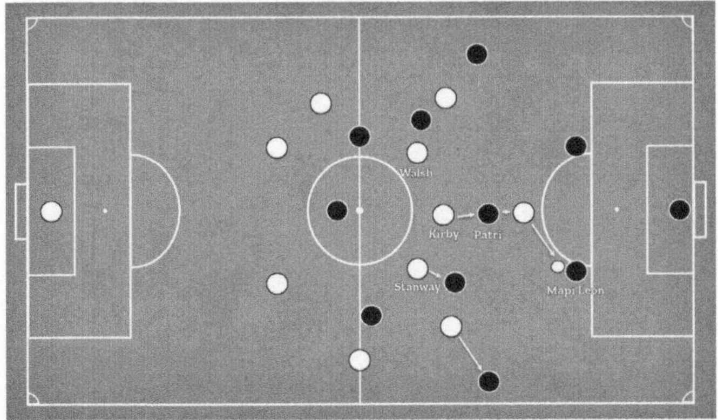

[Figure 16]

Here, England's trigger to press is when Spain started advancing to just before the halfway line. White would start hovering around the ball carrier but the shift really came once León or Paredes needed to make the next pass. Either Kirby or Stanway would block off the passing lanes to Guijarro to ensure Spain opted for longer-range passes. This style of press brings the compactness principle into play. They knew man-marking Spain high up the pitch wouldn't work, so they needed to hold shape and ensure there were no

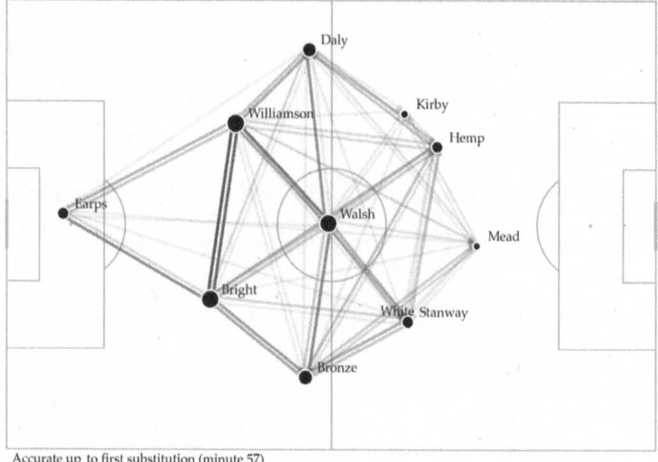

[Figure 17]

easy passing lanes. Stop the ball into Guijarro, and Spain have to play longer switches to the wide areas or riskier passes into Bonmatí or Teresa Abelleira. ***Figure 17*** is England's pass map – notice Walsh's positioning as it's visibly higher than normal, with Kirby and Stanway in obviously wider positions to stop Spain's midfield from easy turn and passes.

So far, so good. Theoretically, England's plan to remain compact and to press based on certain triggers meant they would try and win back possession and counterattack, but Spain still managed to bypass their press and found an effective way of exposing the one obvious area of weakness – the full-backs.

Limit the press and supply

Vilda knew his side were superior in recycling possession. Being able to keep the ball and repurpose it in short, calculated passes meant they were able to keep England away. Restricting England's potent pressing structure meant they'd have to adjust and limit their use of their full-backs and wingers in counterattacking situations.

Spain's 4-1-4-1 was designed to create numerical superiority across the thirds. The flexibility of Bonmatí and Abelleira meant the system would interchange and entice striker Esther González to not only drop deep and interchange play, but to make runs in behind as well. The challenge was for Spain to find a solution to England's aggressive wide pressing sequence without losing possession in the next phase of play.

Spain's response carried two solutions: the first was to get their best ball carriers in a position to receive, collect, and play their way out given their superior positional awareness and movement; the second was to attempt quick passing combinations through England's compact shape to try and use the spaces that were left open to their advantage. Each of these solutions would provide Wiegman and England with a different problem to tackle and for 80 minutes, it worked.

Vilda resorted to four different midfield combinations in the tournament, but it was the current one that seemed to synergise and work in tandem with the players around them. Abelleira, Bonmatí, and Guijarro are excellent ball carriers and using them as the conduits to walk into the line of fire and play their way out worked. Bonmatí marshalled the midfield while Guijarro assumed the role of deputy where both players dictated how Spain would manoeuvre their plays. Abelleira was the foot soldier who followed orders and kept play ticking with a composed presence in the middle. She was where she needed to be, and that's all Spain needed from the *Blaugrana* midfielder.

The 42nd minute had a passage of play where I probably witnessed one of the most coherent and elegant moves in football. This sequence in ***Figure 18***

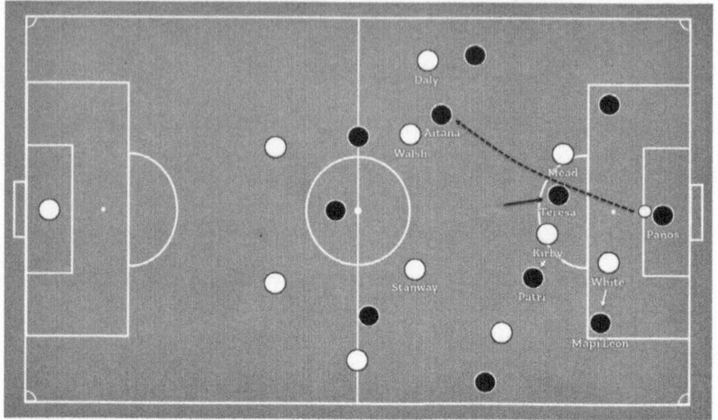

[Figure 18]

was one where Spain played out of England's press from a goal kick. The passage of play started with an exchange between goalkeeper Sandra Paños and Mapi León with White changing tack and pressing the centre-back higher up the pitch. While Kirby was cover-shadowing Guijarro, Abelleira recognised this and dropped in to create a double pivot, putting Kirby off Guijarro and having to split focus between the two midfielders.

The ball eventually made its way to Spain's right, getting played into Bonmatí. Walsh, Hemp, Daly, and Kirby all surrounded the diminutive midfielder who then played a one-two pass sequence with Guijarro before progressing it forward, forcing England to retreat and allowing Bonmatí to switch play out to Olga Carmona – the left-back – in space on the left.

Movements and sequences such as this empowered Spain to play with dominance and freedom and put England on the back foot. The passing sequences are seamlessly integrated into these moves. The DNA of Spain and Barcelona are distinctly different from each other; however, at their core, they both involve intricate passing and variety in movement. The Spanish ranked highest in build-ups with 20 according to website The Analyst, with England just behind them on 19. This insistence on playing out from the back only comes from confidence and consideration to use the strengths of their nexus.

A passing exchange and sequence in the 17th minute was a glimpse of how rapidly Spain can move the ball from back to front. Paredes received the ball after a spell of pressure from England but Spain managed to find a way out of that situation. The centre-back quickly passed out to the dropping González before laying it off to Abelleira in the half-space. Abelleira took one touch to then play Caldentey in, out in the wide areas in space once again. Om Arvind describes Spain's movements and the impact their individuals had on the collective:

'There are many different ways of describing press resistance and analysts tend to focus on the collective – the structure in possession, certain off-ball movements, and passing patterns. But, arguably, at its most fundamental, a team's ability to beat pressure comes down to each individual duel. There can be no successful third-player/third-man run (however you want to phrase it) if the player on the ball fails to seek out a yard of space and open up a passing angle, whether that be through a clever shoulder drop or deceptive touch.

'It was this individual superiority that Aitana Bonmatí and Patri Guijarro gifted Spain. Even when the structure was off or the support suspect, Aitana would slyly do a 360 with the ball before jetting off, dizzying her marker, and breaking the press. Patri might not have been so elaborate, but she was similarly slippery, always taking the right touch at the right moment to create space.'

The main problem for England here was that Walsh and Stanway were being pulled out of position by the fluid movements of the Spanish attacking number eights and though in possession the Lionesses seemed comfortable, Spain were wary of blocking the passes into the pivot players. England were late in adjusting to the change and eventually moving to the 3-4-3 enabled them to hold possession better and create better opportunities to play out. The underlying solution for Spain lay within: you stop the source, you stop England from functioning.

Off the ball, the first 25 minutes saw Spain look to press England high and not allow Walsh much time in possession. Similar to the role Guijarro plays for Spain, Walsh is an enigma given her deceptively innocuous playing style, yet she is England's most intelligent ball progressor and, in my opinion, central to England's team as a whole. Limiting the supply to Walsh meant England did not have a pressure valve when the wide areas were off-limits as any build-up sequence relied on

Walsh being available to play wall passes into Bronze or Daly. Spain's recognition of this was obvious as the game wore on.

One moment in the 20th minute saw both González and Bonmatí press Walsh as she received a pass from a throw-in. This routine set piece was an opportunity for Spain to step forward and stop play from progressing, and though Walsh managed to slip away, putting two players in to press – even if opportunistically – showed the intent of stopping England's *regista*.

In both examples, Spain utilised their strengths. Spain play in a very aggressive and expansive way, throwing both full-backs forward and deploying their own *regista* ahead of two centre-backs, and in doing so they need to dominate the ball. Their high-octane style also comes with the drawbacks of leaving space behind the full-backs with only two centre-backs left to protect them. However, they also used this to their advantage against England's potency in the wide areas, leading us to point number two.

Focus on the full-backs

The majority of England's success in the tournament prior to this game was their insistence on using Mead, Hemp, Bronze, and Daly as their attacking and defensive outlets. The four players played a crucial role in transitioning England on to the front foot, giving them a higher base to start with. When opposition build-up is forced into the wide spaces, the full-back and winger will squeeze and suffocate the space for the ball carrier by hurrying them into a mistake or dispossessing them higher up the pitch.

Spain realised they needed to capitalise on the full-backs' dangerously high positioning. They knew that if they could keep the pressure on Bronze and Daly they would limit the damage they could inflict, both in attacking and defending. Equally, if not, more importantly, they had to stop Mead and Hemp from laying waste to the flanks and win their individual battles. Using Olga Carmona and Ona Batlle became more than just a means of stopping England but a rather potent attacking weapon as well, which yielded good results.

When England did manage to get into a position that pushed Spain back into their own half, they were able to spray passes around to try and break down the Spanish shape and they had their moments. In such situations, the Spanish full-backs needed to be positionally perfect and ensure they won their one-on-one duels against the wingers.

Here in ***Figure 19,*** Spain revert back into a closely lined 4-2-3-1 defensive shape. Bright breaks the first line and finds a spot to play a line-breaking pass

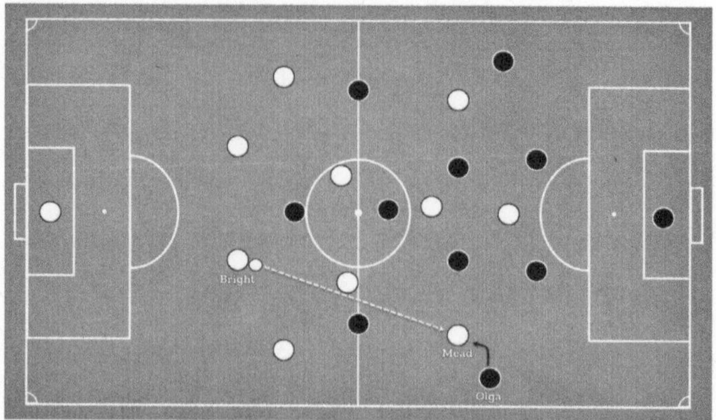

[Figure 19]

through to Mead on the right flank. The Arsenal winger is now on the ascendency and is in a clear one-on-one duel with Carmona. The Real Madrid left-back's speed and body positioning gave her the chance to keep track of Mead's movement and to adjust to her change of pace. The result ended with Carmona winning the battle and dispossessing Mead, and subsequently saw Spain play a string of passes out from the back.

Wiegman made a big call to select Daly as her starting left-back, given the presence in the squad of Alex Greenwood and Demi Stokes, who are more natural choices in the position. Daly's use as a left-back is an asset and she brings qualities that suit Wiegman's transition structure; however, in a pure defensive situation, wingers will relish the chance to come up against the Aston Villa striker.

Though there is a distinct drawback to England's full-backs, teams weren't able to take full advantage of it and I'll rationalise my thoughts on the matter later in the book. For this match, some of Daly's positioning choices and decisions in one-on-one duels exposed her as a left-back. She played pretty well against Marta Cardona who started the game on the right wing, but her struggles really began when Athenea del Castillo came on. The diminutive winger is an eccentric and electric presence on the flank and her ability to drive either side of the full-back is immense. The unpredictability of her movements caused Daly many problems, even laying her on the floor on a couple of occasions.

Spain changed their point of attack by making their switches of play from the left to right to leave Athenea isolated with Daly just as England themselves do with Hemp. A couple of moments in the second half saw Athenea almost score from an attempt out wide, but it was the subsequent play that forced England into making a change.

Figure 20 is a representation of this move, which in isolation isn't what caused the substitution; rather it was the trigger after a series of battles that brought Greenwood on. Here, Athenea picks up the ball and runs towards Daly, forcing her back towards her own

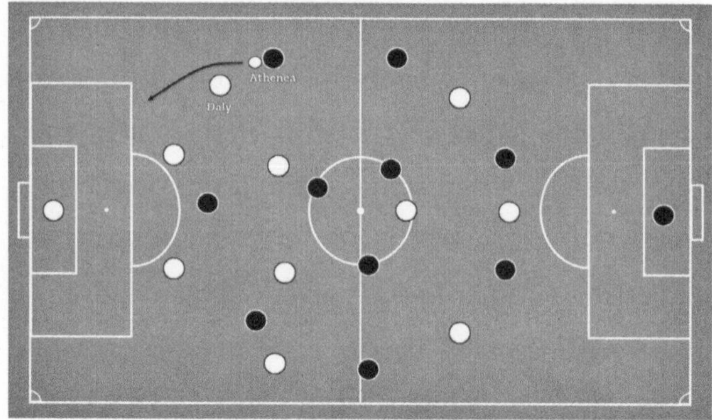

[Figure 20]

box, and in an instant drives to her outside, playing a threatening cross in. The resulting move finally saw the ball in Mary Earps's hand but the threat she brought was undeniable.

England's response to Spain's dominance was to switch to a 3-4-3 and resort to plan B, which was to play Bright as a centre-forward. By playing a more recognised wing-back and getting more superiority in the wide areas, England overloaded Spain to change their focus.

> *'Russo's arrival made a huge difference in this game. She closed down relentlessly and bullied Irene Paredes in the air, causing panic in the Spanish penalty box. Wiegman had Hemp and Kelly on their "weaker" sides, cutting in and crossing in-swingers towards Russo. Ella Toone*

would hover in support, looking for second balls. Eventually, Millie Bright joined Russo up front, and Spain could no longer cope with England's direct play.'

– Blair Newman

The resulting move paid dividends as it allowed a wide cross from Hemp from the right into a crowd of Spanish defenders and Russo headed it back towards Toone to score the equaliser. Wiegman reverted to type with England back to their 4-3-3 system, and they dominated extra time. Stanway's goal came from a direct run forward and a retreating Spain left enough space for the Bayern midfielder to unleash a venomous shot to win it.

Tenacious or lucky?

Spain's game plan was near perfect. They showed other teams where England could be threatened and, in some regard, can be considered unlucky not to have scored more during the 90 minutes. England survived and the change to a 3-4-3 late in the second half, itself prompted by the Greenwood substitution and activation of plan B by moving Bright as a centre-forward, subsequently saw them vastly improve by scoring the equaliser and later the winner from Stanway.

Were England just lucky, or did their tenacity and Wiegman's tactical switches do the trick? You would have to say it was a bit of both given the chances Spain had to double their lead but England capitalised on those misses by making suitable changes and using their impact players wisely.

There was a visible improvement with the formation change, but there was an inevitability of other teams exploiting the midfield build-up. The solution to this problem lies within the same midfield in the form of Keira Walsh and how she dealt with the dilemma posed by Sweden proves as much.

Chapter 7

Sweden – the triumph of the metronome

'Keira Walsh was instrumental to England's midfield. She determined build-up shape, drew pressure and opposition players with excellent composure. Keira was one of the conductors of Georgia's [Stanway] movements which organised the midfield setup.'

– Willie Kirk

THE AFTERMATH of the quarter-final win over Spain was met with much excitement and assuredness. What started out as a hopeful dream was now slowly transforming into an attainable reality. England were just one match away from reaching an international final, their most significant accomplishment yet after three past semi-final appearances. But standing in their way was a giant of European football and one of the tournament's favourites in Sweden.

The Swedes were billed as 'the ones to beat'. They arguably had one of the most cohesive and strongest squads that had bulldozed their way through the Olympics a year earlier, only to be beaten by Canada in the final. Every major tournament sees Peter Gerhardsson's side threaten to come away as champions, yet they've fallen short each time. In some quarters this was seen as the final chance for the Swedes to achieve silverware with this crop of players, a golden generation if you will. But the Euros didn't exactly go to plan with several Covid-19 cases disrupting their momentum, which forced Gerhardsson into multiple changes during the group stage and quarter-finals.

Despite all the obstacles thrown in their way, Sweden were still a formidable opponent and England needed to be worried about their attacking threat. If there's one point about the Swedes that makes them so hard to beat, it is their solid structure and the consistency of their players. While they didn't make too many changes to the overall system, they were incredibly well-drilled in what they knew. I broke down the quarter-final in the previous chapter and explained how Spain were able to break down England, but at one point in this game it seemed like Sweden were able to do a little bit more.

So why was it that after 90 minutes of the semi-final, England came out 4-0 victors in what would seem like an entirely dominant performance? Anyone that watched the game will know that Sweden's first 25 minutes were promising and exploited England more than any other side had done before.

Gerhardsson's plan

Sweden came out with a set and structured game plan from the outset. Gerhardsson's atypical high-pressing game suited the nature of the tie and had what was required to find solutions against a rampant England side. Going up against a team that has a set method of playing out from the back with four competent ball players meant Sweden's pressing structure had to be on point.

Wiegman's team had shown some signs of disparity against Spain, who disrupted their pressing scheme and were able to repel their build-up mechanics. By taking the parts of the blueprint from that game and in their own impressive structure, Sweden carefully crafted a plan to deter England's flow and movement patterns.

Sweden's tactical plan was indicated from their starting line-up. Gerhardsson began with his usual

4-2-3-1 formation where he made a slight change in the back line with Hanna Glas, Magdalena Eriksson, Linda Sembrant, and Amanda Ilestedt starting. Glas is a natural right-back playing at left-back while Ilestedt is a centre-back playing at right-back. The idea was to curtail two of England's focal points in Lauren Hemp and Beth Mead. Further forward they had Nathalie Björn and Filippa Angeldahl settling in as the double pivot behind a front four of Fridolina Rolfö, Kosovare Asllani, Sofia Jakobsson, and Stina Blackstenius.

The two defensive midfielders would ensure the central-third supply into Keira Walsh and Georgia Stanway was stunted and if England did get through, the pair would act as two screens in front of the back four. Björn is another natural defender playing in a defensive midfield position while Angeldahl is a box-to-box creative midfielder. The two in tandem would ensure that Sweden were physical and agile enough in defensive transitions but also equally effective in attacking transitions to support the front five.

The attacking players were selected for their off-the-ball work and creativity. Asllani is the fulcrum of their attacking line-up and is the one who dictates the tempo, so she was given the task of man-marking Walsh. The speed and precision of Blackstenius and Rolfö were enough to confirm their places, but it was the selection of Jakobsson that raised a few eyebrows. The San Diego Wave winger had hardly had a look in until this game.

Given Sweden's use of Lina Hurtig as the central striker and Blackstenius on the wing, it made sense to bring in a more recognised wide player like Johanna Rytting Kaneryd.

Nonetheless, the inclusion of Jakobsson was understood quickly given how she settled into the game plan. Instead of using Hurtig as a target striker, utilising more pace and one-on-one artists across the front line meant they could isolate and target England's defenders.

> *'Sweden should have started Johanna Rytting Kaneryd over Sofia Jakobsson. [Kaneryd] could have caused England's full-backs more problems given their weaknesses there. Her directness and ability to drive at players deserved more minutes.'*
>
> **– Alina Ruprecht**

Controlled pressing to attack the channels

Just as how the Spain game had started, Sweden wanted to control England's build-up. Their method of doing this was by controlling their press through a man-marking system where special care was given to stop the central pivot: Keira Walsh. Walsh's importance to England is clear but before diving into her adjustments, it's important to understand that Sweden made it a point to stop England from building out through their full-backs as a priority.

When Williamson and Bright received the initial pass, their options to go wide were limited given how high Sweden's wingers were positioned in such a way as to bait England into passing into Rachel Daly and Lucy Bronze. Any time they attempted passes out wide, the ball would be played back. They weren't allowed to play quickly between them, and the Swedes ensured the passing lanes were covered. Sweden's 4-4-1-1 pressing shape left one centre-back free to move with the striker marking the other while the others were covered by the rest.

This was seen in just the third minute as I've illustrated in ***Figure 21*** where Sweden lined up in

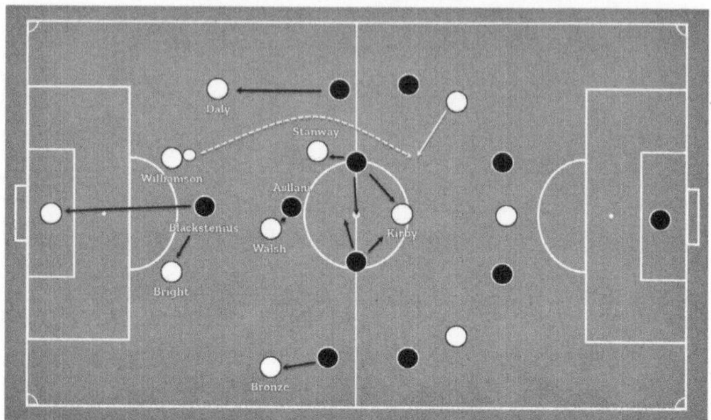

[Figure 21]

the aforementioned shape with Blackstenius cover-shadowing Bright and Mary Earps, Asllani marking Walsh, and so on. Williamson received possession in space but had no real passing options except for stepping forward into the vacant space. With the double pivot blocking passes to Stanway and Kirby, the Arsenal captain really had no clear options. Though she opted for a longer pass here, it required Hemp to drop in between the lines into a crowd of players, resulting in a reset. England had to go back and start their build-up process again.

> *'For 20 odd minutes, it looked like Sweden were on top. Kosovare Asllani was paying special attention to Keira Walsh, sinking so far back on her that Leah Williamson had a good ten yards to eat up before being engaged. This scheme disrupted England's rhythm and allowed Sweden to control the flow of proceedings, which led to incisive, coordinated attacks behind Lucy Bronze.'*
>
> **– Om Arvind**

This constant structured press from Sweden meant England were controlled and finding a way into Kirby or Stanway was becoming increasingly difficult. The Lionesses' tempo had always remained high and in most fixtures, their control over the pace of the game dictated their penetration through the thirds. Sweden's rigid structure meant they weren't able to control possession in their intended areas, thus playing into Sweden's plan of slowing things down.

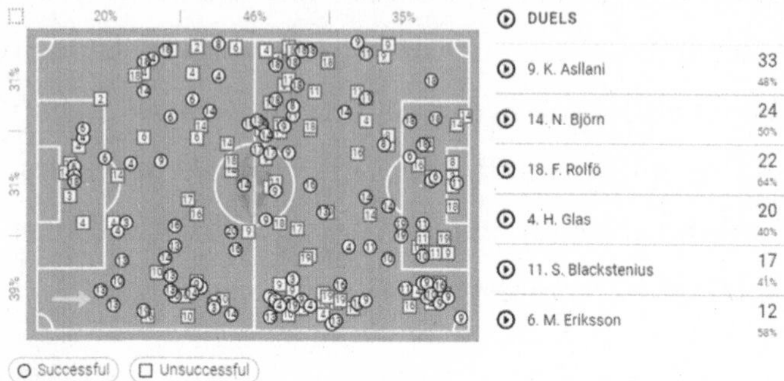

[Figure 22]

Figure 22 is Sweden's duel map, which pinpoints every area they engaged. Keeping the duels in the penalty area aside, the majority of their engagements took place just outside the box and on both flanks in slightly deeper positions. The wingers winning the ball back in these areas meant they limited the English full-backs from entering the final third while enticing the wingers to drop deep to receive. Win the ball back here, and space behind the English full-backs opens up for Swedish wide players to exploit. Rolfö and Jakobsson had to be disciplined out of possession and when the opportunities arose, they could combine with Blackstenius – who expertly ran the channels – to create clear-cut chances.

If we focus on the area outside of the penalty box, then we know that Sweden were trying to derail England's bid to allow Walsh and Stanway to receive possession. A lot of England's connecting play between the defensive and final thirds comes from the pivot, specifically Walsh. The Manchester City midfielder is an elite ball carrier and visionary who controls England's tempo. By having someone man-mark her, you effectively remove a pressure valve and force England to go long which gave Sweden a much better chance of winning back possession.

Gerhardsson used Asllani as the marker. The Milan striker was played as a number ten and was effectively cover-shadowing and pressing Walsh out of possession to prevent any passes from coming into her. Here in ***Figure 23***, we see an example of this in action. Around the 20th minute, Sweden moved into a 4-4-1-1 system that had Blackstenius pressure the centre-back without the ball (in this example Williamson) and Asllani marking Walsh. Bright was left with very few options given how Daly and Bronze were being cover-shadowed by the wingers, and any attempt to pass to any of them gave enough time for the Swedish wide players to react and press. The eventual diagonal

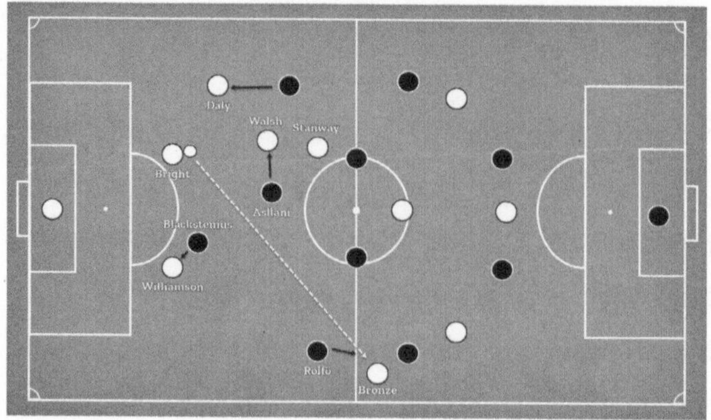

[Figure 23]

pass out to an advancing Bronze was quickly covered and won back by Rolfö.

These pressing tactics had an end game which was to counter and release the attacking players into the vacant spaces that were left behind and around England's defensive line.

One of Sweden's main limitations has been against low-block teams, given the lack of fluidity from the central midfield duo in their 4-2-3-1. In the past, we've seen Caroline Seger and Angeldahl played for their defensive steel but against England, they would be the ones sitting deep and counterattacking. This is the exact type of game that Gerhardsson wanted and would have suited his attacking players. Having this base to cover their pressing out of possession also meant the attacking players could push on without the threat of being exposed in behind.

In Rolfö and Jakobsson, Sweden had players able to run in behind and take advantage of space. So far, we've talked about the space behind England's full-backs ad nauseam and in the first 15 minutes, Sweden were able to execute phase one of their grand master plan. When England did push up, Sweden were able to win the ball back and use speed to isolate the centre-backs before runners made their way into the box. ***Figure 24*** is a case from very early on in the match where Sweden capitalised on this.

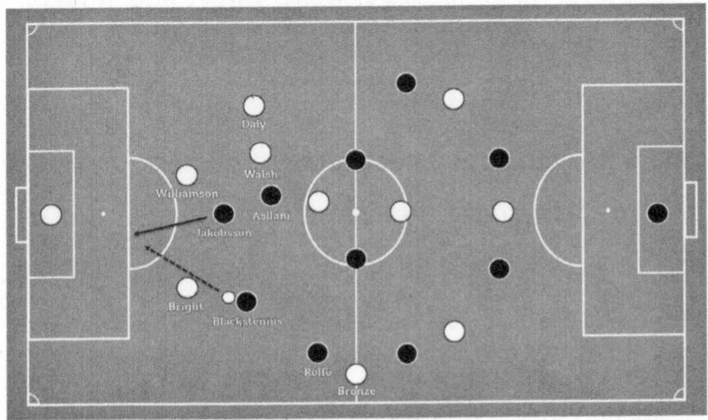

[Figure 24]

Sweden successfully pressed England right from the kick-off and dispossessed Stanway around the halfway line. England's full-backs were pushed up and the turnover put Sweden in a four-v-three situation. When Blackstenius picked up the ball, she was in behind Bronze and played in Jakobsson who made a run across from right to left to catch Bright by surprise. She took a shot that was saved by Earps but their intent had been signalled in the opening seconds.

> *'The downfall of Sweden came from players playing out of position. Gerhardsson's decisions seemed to work for the first 15 minutes but failing to take their chances gave England a route back.'*
>
> **– Alina Ruprecht**

This wasn't the only attack; it just shows how England were put on the back foot from the very start. In retaliation, England had Stanway drop to create a double pivot in an attempt to disrupt and move Sweden's forward press, creating a numerical advantage in the defensive third which was when the game started getting away from them. Nonetheless, even with a second midfielder dropping in to become a double pivot, it was the intelligence and adjustments of England's single pivot player that made all the difference.

The Walsh effect

> *'Keira Walsh is a different type of number six to Lena Oberdorf but a perfect number six in her own style.'*
>
> **– Willie Kirk**

As is customary with Sarina Wiegman, she made adjustments on the fly and once again the key to this was the movement and positioning of Keira Walsh. The initial problem was Walsh being marked out of the game after being pressured and pressed by Asllani. The way England solved this was by almost removing her from the equation in the initial build-up phase.

Wiegman recognised that Sweden's structure catered to crowding the defensive third area outside the box, and she had to find a way to get the ball into midfield by bypassing the four in midfield. Part of the solution came with Stanway dropping in to become a true number six next to Walsh to create an extra body but more importantly, it was Walsh side-stepping Asllani and moving out of the central passing lane.

The 25-year-old is a rare talent who encapsulates an almost 'anti-English' style of play. Walsh is probably the only current English player with the elegance and poise that embodies someone from a Spanish footballing institution – the English metronome. Walsh's constant scanning and lightning-quick reactions are key to her having a 360-degree view of her surroundings. She never switches off and has the inherent tactical understanding and mental agility to decipher multiple options and choose the best one. On top of that, she possesses an excellent range of passing that is supported by an 86.6 per cent accuracy rate in her England career.

> *'Walsh tends to fly under the radar. But make no mistake, she is no shrinking violet. Walsh's quiet dominance in the middle when playing for Barcelona is unparalleled, and her ability to pinpoint a ball to a run is quite unique. Walsh is the ultimate playmaker and should not be underestimated.'*
>
> **– Charlotte Stacey**

By slightly adjusting her positioning on the pitch, she was able to move Asllani out of position just enough to provide space for Kirby or Stanway to drop deep and central to receive longer passes from Williamson. By adapting to Sweden's press, England knew they couldn't play short passes out from the back so they converted their seemingly forced option into a positive, which we can see an example of in ***Figure 25***.

This sequence came from a throw-in to Sweden which England won back easily and started their build-up process from. The pass to Walsh and then Williamson saw England start out from the back again with Asllani tailing the Barcelona midfielder. Now, once the England captain got on the ball, Walsh started

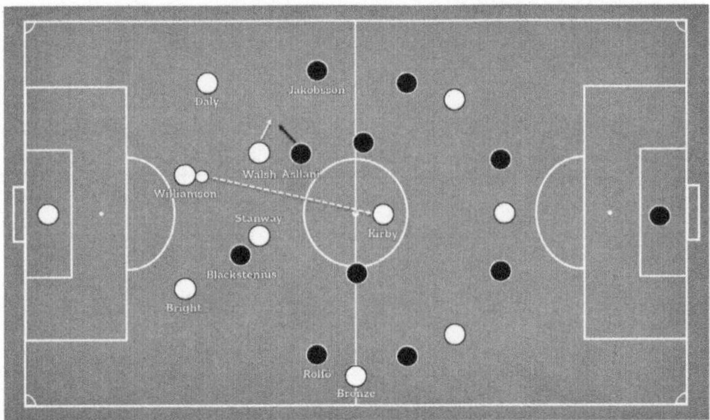

[Figure 25]

to move ever so slightly to her left and Stanway dropped to be in line with Walsh and moved to her right.

These movements caused a bit of hesitancy for both Asllani and Björn, who were caught in two minds on whether to cover the passing lane or the player. The split-second thinking time enabled Williamson to play a direct, low pass to Kirby, who received possession in the centre circle and turned to move forward. She won her duel with Björn and suddenly England had possession in the final third without resorting to chance through long passes.

This, in turn, put pressure on Sweden to readjust their tactics, moving players out of position. Given how compact and strict their structure was, having to shift the central midfield players to step up became a liability as it left space for Kirby in between the lines. If we pinpoint Walsh's received passes as defined in

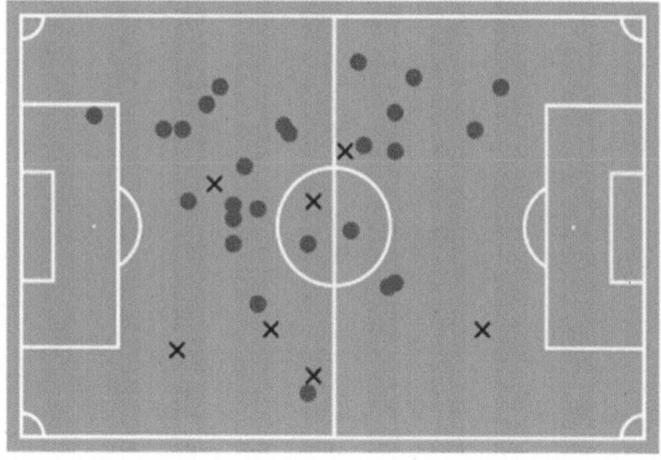

● Won ✕ Lost

[Figure 26]

Figure 26, you can see that the vast majority of those passes were taken in the left defensive half-space. This implies that Walsh spent a lot of her time in that area of the pitch which gave England the capacity to build more effectively.

> *'Few teams in the world have been able to handle Peter Gerhardsson's 4-4-1-1 defensive structure historically, with even the USWNT [USA] famously struggling multiple times – including in their humiliating 3-0 loss in the 2021 Olympics. It's that fact that forcefully puts into context Keira Walsh's quality, with*

England solving one of the toughest tactical problems of the tournament as a result of her movement.

'By dropping into the left half-space, Walsh dragged Asllani aside and opened up a lane into Georgia Stanway, who reacted by forming a double pivot. If Sweden's midfield didn't react, Stanway was free. If they did, Kirby was left one-on-one with the full width of the pitch to manoeuvre.

'Thus, while each midfielder played their part, it all started with Walsh – as everything with England tends to.'

– Om Arvind

The resulting situations enabled Walsh to control England's play slightly higher up the pitch. Given that I've talked about play being more direct with players dropping deeper to collect, any time the attack had to 'reset', the ball would be played back to a higher starting position where Walsh had much more room to dictate. The intuitiveness in Walsh's cognitive intelligence relates to how she's able to find the best options more often than not. She creates more time for herself than she's been afforded, which gives her more time to make decisions. The relationship between ball and player couldn't be more in sync and the numerous times we saw her attempt line-breaking passes to break the opposition's defensive structure was further evidence of this.

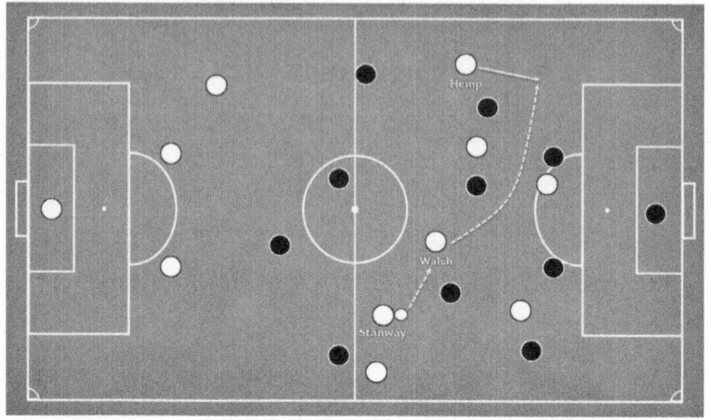

[Figure 27]

Figure 27 is a situation where England managed to play out from the back successfully and push their entire line forward. The drive from Stanway down the right and her inside pass to Walsh was met with a first-time ball down to Hemp on the left. This one-instant hit seemed like a no-look pass and to most other players it might have been a lucky delivery, but Walsh's scanning ability to know where every player is on the pitch at every moment assures us that it's all down to skill.

Battle for supremacy

So far, the theme of Wiegman's England is the contributions coming from key individual players to create solutions to specific problems that then have a ripple effect on the collective. On this day it was Keira Walsh's small yet significant contribution that changed the dynamic of England's build-up worries. If there wasn't enough proof of a well-settled team before, then this game eliminated all doubts. Wiegman's Lionesses had slain Gerhardsson's Valkyries in a battle for supremacy and a final duel against the Germans was all that stood in their way to claiming the throne.

Given that the semi-final had ended with a scoreline of 4-0 to England, one would think the home side catastrophically demolished the opposition. It was, however, to the contrary as the Swedes found a game plan that worked but they had failed to put away any of the early chances that came their way. If they had scored just one of those opportunities then we could have been talking about a completely different game, but in the end, it was England who took their chances and they were one step closer to the finish line.

Chapter 8

Germany – a hope restored

'The final was a gamechanger – not just for England, but also for Germany. It changed the way our nation looks at women's football. It made heroes visible and showed young girls that dreams can come true.'

– Jasmina Schweimler

'IT'S COMING HOME'. The phrase is synonymous with every England team at every major tournament. While its use has traditionally been in jest, the feeling among the fanbase this time round was that it might all come to fruition on 31 July 2022.

This day will go down as one of England's greatest in women's football – scratch that, in English sporting history as a whole. After the men won the 1966 World Cup and the cricketers claimed their global trophy in 2019, the women delivered yet another milestone for the nation – it might just be the most exhilarating one they've had.

An England win at Wembley in front of 87,000 was one of the most invigorating experiences I can ever remember. The days leading up to the final were building with trepidation and the city of London was brimming with excitement. Being cascaded around footballing people, the potential for an intense yet tactical final was mooted among the journalists and analysts.

From the hotel to the stadium, the journey to Wembley was a sea of red and white (or tangerine) with a sense of genuine elation and a realisation that England could win the Euros for the first time. Wembley Way carried a euphoria that was unlike anything I'd ever experienced before. My travelling party were just as enthralled by the atmosphere, and we were eagerly awaiting what promised to be a tactically intriguing battle.

There was heartbreak a year earlier when the men faced Italy at the same stage on the same ground and had been beaten in a penalty shoot-out, but this time there was something about the Lionesses that was capable of more. There was the sense that they could at last overcome that final hurdle. As I made my way up the steps at Wembley, I realised I was experiencing a once-in-a-lifetime opportunity to see England win a tournament.

They entered this final as slight favourites given the home crowd and their resounding wins so far. However, Germany weren't far off and a tactically astounding win against France in the semi-final showed they had the acumen and nous to outwit savvy opposition. Both teams showed dominance and a threatening aura and now came the game to show who was the best.

Germany's pedigree speaks for itself. They're eight-time European champions, two-time World Cup winners, and have won Olympic gold. More importantly, they're a team that knows how to win. Coming into the tournament they were dismissed as only potential winners – not 'serious' contenders. As they progressed through their group and beat Austria in the quarter-finals, the onlookers started to take notice of the Germans' performances. Their squad brimmed with immense talent, ranging from the multiple wonderkids to the heavily experienced veterans.

Lena Oberdorf is considered the best young talent in world football by many and arguably the best defensive midfielder of her generation. The Wolfsburg player performed at another level in this tournament and remained a key component in the final. Alexandra Popp, in contrast, was the experienced figurehead who came in when Lea Schüller tested positive for Covid before the opening match. From that point on her inclusion was billed as a blessing in disguise as she found herself the tournament's joint top scorer alongside England's Beth Mead.

A last-minute warm-up injury to Popp meant she was replaced by the player whom she herself replaced in Schüller. That was the beginning of an intriguing tactical battle given how crucial the Wolfsburg striker was to Germany's style of play. A point of reference was removed and how England were able to capitalise on this became their sole focus. Popp gave Germany a different dimension and they were able to build a side around her physicality, which is a point I will reference in further detail later in the book.

Sarina Wiegman and Martina Voss-Tecklenburg conjured tactical masterclasses en route to the final. Seeing who would come out on top and find ways to exploit the deficiencies both teams displayed throughout the tournament would be the ultimate surprise. At 5pm local time the final kicked off, and we sat back to watch the madness unfold.

German efficiency

The German approach to the final was intuitive and effective, to say the least. Voss-Tecklenburg's mentality has always been very much focused on a possession-savvy game plan that has a particular emphasis on the wings with the wide forwards as their main source of creativity.

Germany's supply and build-up are centrally focused using positional rotations and combinations from the full-backs coming inside to create interior combination plays, with Popp as the target striker who brings this all together.

All of this is confined to a 4-3-3 system that Voss-Tecklenburg uses to create turnovers and ensure the quick, wide players are given acres of space to drive into. Diving further into the dynamics of the system, their attacking build-up comes from the right-hand side with Svenja Huth and Lina Magull drifting into the half-spaces to create passing combinations.

The two interchange positions to a degree as Huth likes to drop deep to collect possession and Magull replaces her as an attacking wide player. Generally, she sits in the half-space to attack but these combination plays are what make Germany an unpredictable force. To add to this, Giulia Gwinn's unorthodox role at right full-back sees her make numerous interior runs and create an extra body in midfield which allows one of Magull or Sara Däbritz to push forward to become an extra attacker.

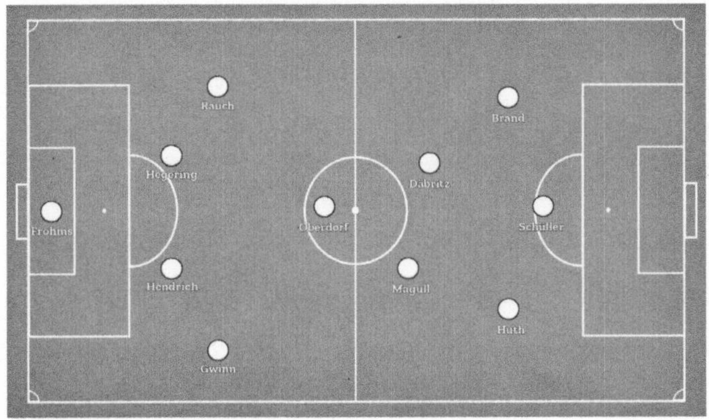

[Figure 28]

On the opposite side, Klara Bühl is a more natural left-sided forward who wants to hug the touchline in the early progression phase but is still keen to attack the back post or even play in one-on-one situations to take on her full-back. The Bayern Munich winger is electric in the wide areas and Voss-Tecklenburg's insistence on having two one-on-one artists – who are optimal at both the progression and attacking phases of play respectively – means they are well-suited to not just their general possession-based game but also a turnover one. ***Figure 28*** is a graphic depicting the basic movement principles expected from Voss-Tecklenburg and where she wanted these players to be moving.

What's most important to highlight is how Germany's midfield is the fulcrum and control centre, particularly Oberdorf. The default triumvirate is Magull, Däbritz, and Oberdorf, but it's the latter who dictates and controls the defensive and attacking transitions, especially in high-pressure situations.

Oberdorf plays as the single pivot but controls the area as a double pivot on her own. Her intelligence enables her to break up play and, more importantly, anticipate the upcoming plays. Scanning and understanding positional play and player positions are her forte that enables Oberdorf to be as good as she is.

Germany's 4-5-1 off-ball structure sees the wide players drop deep and block passing lanes, triggering a high-pressing sequence. They were the highest-pressing team of the tournament, ending with 158 pressing sequences registered. In the progression phase, Oberdorf creates space for the other two number eights to play a bit more freely and protect the back four from being overly exposed. The forward forays of Felicitas Rauch and Gwinn's inside runs leave a need for someone to cover the spaces in behind them, which Oberdorf seems to be perfectly placed to do in attacking scenarios.

A good example is Oberdorf's performance against Austria, where this sort of counterattacking situation posed a threat. One passage of play against Austria saw a ball ricochet off a German player after Oberdorf was able to intercept a loose touch from an Austrian player earlier in the move. The ricochet was anticipated early by Oberdorf, putting herself in a position to recognise potential danger and react accordingly.

Her true value comes in defensive transitions where she's able to almost single-handedly halt attacks on her own. If Germany are caught on their heels and have just two centre-backs plus Oberdorf, then she's able to ascertain the situation and make the right decision. It helps that she's a physical specimen, but you need the brains to back the athleticism and Oberdorf does just that.

'Oberdorf's constant scanning and lightning reaction time are key to fostering the impression that she is everywhere. She never switches off and has the processing speeds, inherent tactical understanding, and mental agility to track multiple threats and determine which one is the most dangerous.'

– Om Arvind

Popp's role is interesting and only came to light under peculiar circumstances. Voss-Tecklenburg needed to adjust Germany's attacking trio to accommodate Popp, but it ultimately transformed the whole team in such a way that they needed to reorient to the Wolfsburg striker. Voss-Tecklenburg used Popp as a reference point and ensured play was driven towards her to then attract defenders to create one-on-one situations for the wide players.

Both Bühl and Huth want the space to attack and bringing her in allowed Germany to have a player intelligent in close quarters but also to present an aerial option. In either scenario, Popp could play in the two wide forwards and this ultimately gave them the edge. Defenders just couldn't cope with the combination play of the front three and Popp ended up as the joint top scorer, which meant the experiment turned out to be a rousing success.

This system worked against every type of opposition they encountered and though adjustments were made, just like they were against France, Germany were nonetheless able to retain their key principles of compactness, wide spatial movements, and efficient transitions.

How England handled Schüller and co

When news of Popp's withdrawal from the starting XI filtered through, it suddenly changed the entire dynamic of the game and bringing Schüller back into the mix gave England a slight advantage. Defending against a premier and physical striker brings about its own challenges, but Popp's form and versatility would have forced Bright and Williamson to defend differently. They would have undoubtedly adapted, but it's no secret that it was a massive boost to their chances. Bühl was also left out of the starting XI due to illness but Jule Brand is more of a like-for-like replacement, so it didn't really change much in terms of the quality of personnel.

Both Bright and Williamson bring their own advantages as a central defensive duo. Bright is an excellent box defender while Williamson anticipates danger diligently. Between them, they're able to administer calm to England's back line but their ability to perform well stems from the midfield. If they position themselves well, their job is made a lot easier. The way England adapted to Germany's change in approach made for an interesting watch.

Germany's approach switched from playing a more target-focused, deep-lying build-up game to a more line-breaking one that still kept an element of dropping into midfield. What I mean by this is that Voss-Tecklenburg used Schüller as a hybrid deep connector and line-breaking forward. The goal was to use Schüller in a similar way to the way Sweden had used Stina Blackstenius, though the make-up of the forward line was quite different. Instead of two direct wide players, Germany's line is made up of one incredibly direct inside-forward and one mazy playmaker. A lot of the early game was focused on rotations in the final third and Schüller dropping in to create an extra body in midfield.

Germany applied a 4-4-2 off the ball and to some extent on it too. The attacking shape morphed between a 4-4-2 and 4-2-3-1 with Magull and sometimes Däbritz making runs through the middle. The overcrowded central area meant England needed to deal with the transitions to ensure they were not overrun and exposed to unnecessary overloads. Wiegman stuck to her 4-2-3-1 off-ball structure but asked her double pivot to drop deeper and congest the space between the midfield and defensive line.

The initial success Germany were having was Huth and Magull creating successful passing combinations down the right with Gwinn's impressive hold-up play and timing of passes from right-back. Even with an English defensive midfielder providing support, Germany were able to quickly shift across and effectively use the spaces created in the half-space to break through.

Playing with a single pivot against a team that uses a more fluid front line of players that practically live between the lines meant there was a good chance of being overrun. Walsh isn't a 'destroyer', nor overly mobile, but her footballing intelligence furnishes her with an ability to cover the right spaces early. Wiegman's response to this was to drop Stanway to form the double pivot and ensure she provided extra pressing support in the half-spaces. Additionally, Kirby or the ball-side winger was tasked with cover-shadowing runners from deep. The end result was to ensure there was at the very least an equal number of players to the opposition's to block any potential passing lanes and win individual battles. The full-backs were then more confident in taking on the German wide players and both Daly and Bronze did eventually win some duels.

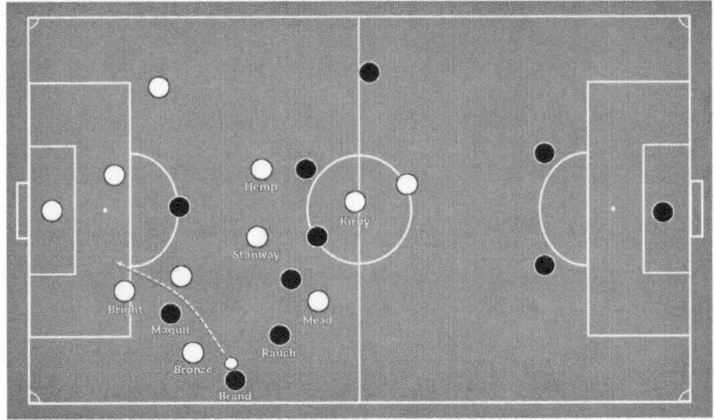

[Figure 29]

Here, ***Figure 29*** is a representation of this concept which came from a passage of play in the first half.

Felicitas Rauch starts another German attack where England were set up with four players between Bright and Kirby's position. As Rauch plays the ball to Brand out on the left, Mead follows the left-back's run across while Brand plays a diagonal grounded pass towards the run of Magull in front of Bright. The pass was just behind Magull, but in this instance, England had players almost man-marking the active German players in the area.

It wasn't just these forward runs they were able to curtail; England equally nullified Schüller's movements into the final third. The change in tactics didn't just make Schüller a player who ran in behind the lines, but one who had to replicate Popp's deeper link-up play. Once she completed her part of the sequence, Schüller would look to drive forward and it was there where the Lionesses were able to nullify the threat.

The shorter distance between England's midfield and defence helped close down the space between the lines for Germany to play in and it gave Williamson and Bright the freedom to press the German attackers before they had a chance to go in behind. A passage of play from the first half saw Brand find herself on the shoulder of the defensive line after Germany took a quick free kick to advance themselves. The midfield and defensive lines maintained a level of closeness with only Brand in between. The pass from Huth towards Brand was anticipated and cut out by Williamson quickly. Throughout the game, England seemed better equipped to deal with these sorts of situations.

If Germany did penetrate the back line, England would rely on the individual quality of their defenders in one-on-one situations to win their duels. A minute before the previous example, Daly was caught in a one-on-one situation against Huth after a Schüller knockdown presented herself with a chance to drive goalwards. The Aston Villa forward managed to block the cross and give England the chance to re-organise.

England's directness with a 4-2-4

Wiegman's introduction of Alessia Russo and Ella Toone pushed England into a 4-2-4 structure with the Manchester United duo as the front two off the ball. Though White's movement did make space for Kirby to play around her, Russo brought a different dynamic that forced Oberdorf to be more cautious and keep Marina Hegering and Kathrin Hendrich engaged. In ***Figure 30*** we can see how this 4-2-4 affected Germany's positioning and how England had more attackers in good attacking positions.

Wiegman's decision to bring on a different striker in Russo and eventually Toone was meant to create

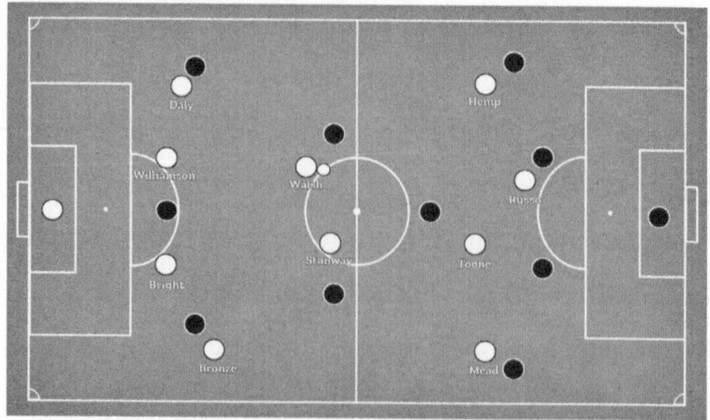

[Figure 30]

more off-the-ball movement and pressing. This is not to say that White isn't a willing presser, but rather Russo's pace and intricate play between the lines became much more effective. Toone brings a varied skillset to the table which is topped off by her ability as the best forward to play on the break, being slightly quicker than Chelsea's Kirby. Toone and Russo play together for Manchester United so their movements and positioning are known to each other. This also gave Wiegman the ability to change formation and use two direct wingers.

Chloe Kelly and Hemp became the wide players and using them as direct enforcers against two tired German full-backs meant they were isolated in one-on-one situations. The entire principle of Wiegman's attacking structure is to give the wingers opportunities to create one-on-one situations and use the central

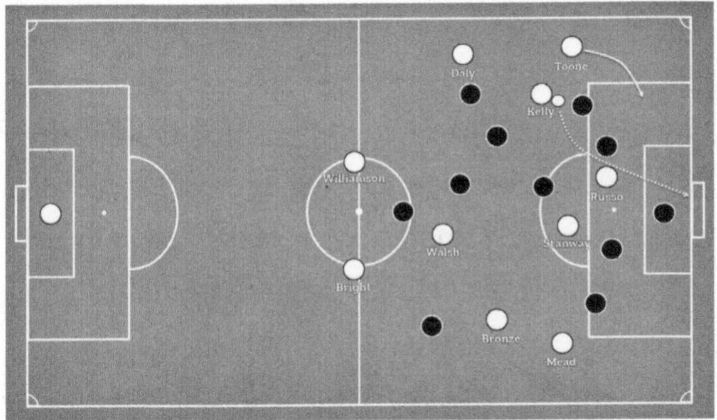

[Figure 31]

players to create depth in the middle. Here, there was more than just the centre-forward in the middle and in Toone and Russo, England now had more power and pace which I've highlighted in ***Figure 31***.

This sequence came at a time when England were dominating possession after Toone's opener. The initial move came from Hemp's driving run down the right flank where she beat Hegering in a one-on-one after taking on Rauch. The resulting cross was just missed, and England then attacked from the left. Daly moved infield and Stanway attracted a couple of players to her position. This left Kelly in a one-on-one position with Toone making an overlapping run. Kelly's drive inside caught Rauch out slightly and Hendrich was too late in stepping forward. Though the resulting shot was saved, it started to give England ball and territorial dominance.

Victory

After 120 minutes, the Lionesses realised the journey of a lifetime. This win not only represented a culmination of Wiegman's management but a whole generation's worth of work. From the days of Hope Powell in 1998 to Phil Neville in 2018, England had been on a quest to build from the ground up. What they achieved by winning the European Championship wasn't just silverware – it cemented a legacy that originated 24 years earlier when Powell was appointed as the first full-time head coach of the national team.

Beating eight-time champions Germany was a statement in and of itself. The road to Australia and New Zealand began long before the Euros, but they now go into the pinnacle of football tournaments, filled with the confidence and belief to go all the way. More tests await the European champions and key personnel will need to be replaced, but Wiegman has delivered something that only a home tournament win can bring in such abundance: hope.

Chapter 9

How does Wiegman use her number tens?

THE NUMBER ten position is one that is considered more fluid than most. Its location and role on the pitch have been debated by many and each coach has their own iteration and vision of it played out. Take Chelsea as an example; they've used both Ji So-Yun and Pernille Harder in varying roles as an advanced, ball-carrying playmaker and shadow striker respectively. Both positions serve different purposes and the use of either is determined by the overall tactics of the side.

More to the point, Germany's use of the number ten is one of the more fluid on the international scene. Their first choice is Lina Magull. Rather than playing in a fixed position, she floats between the lines and lingers in central midfield, interchanging positions and making runs in behind while still being an integral part of the press. Their path to the final relied on the efforts of the collective rather than individuals. The tactics and execution were down to each player carrying out their roles to perfection, and part of that was the importance given to the number ten. This player is now a pivotal part of the coach's overall game plan and philosophy, regardless of if they're played as traditional attacking midfielders or as attacking central midfielders.

In truth, the proper attacking midfielder has faded from the game and even fewer are being used in their natural roles. We've seen the personnel used here referred to as 'luxury' players in the past, and that comes from their willingness to only want to attack and create rather than defend and work hard off the ball. Even players of Vivianne Miedema's or Daniëlle van de Donk's ilk and stature have now begun to play with varying degrees of change, especially when it comes to pressing. The nature of the role has evolved and the modern number ten is expected to be as much of an off-the-ball monster as they are on it.

In essence, explaining the details of the role is simple yet complex. Bear with me as I seek to explain the position's use in England's system in a little more depth before moving on to the role and its personnel. Several attributes can be considered as the foundation of the position, with each iteration bringing its own uniqueness to the table. Positional intelligence and awareness along with out-of-possession movement encourage high levels of chance creation. The role isn't so much about what the player can do on the ball but rather what they can do off it. This natural evolution has followed the incessant need to win high possession turnovers.

To bring this to the point of this chapter, England's use of the number ten isn't as obvious and neither is it orthodox. Sarina Wiegman's version of the position lies in the details, and only upon further analysis does the position becomes much clearer. The core concept is creating overloads in the forward areas while creating an imbalance on one flank with an underload on the opposite. The 4-3-3 setup is very interchangeable, going into a 4-2-3-1 too. The second number eight pushes up to act as a number ten in the attacking phase of possession which prompts the shift to the latter formation.

The role is inherently made to be a supporting operation to facilitate the attacking tendencies of the other forward players while still being a core function. In a sense, Wiegman's attacking midfielder leverages the off-ball work to dictate the on-ball strategy in different phases of play. In transition, the player will hold up play and quickly progress play to try and put the team in good counterattacking positions. Off the ball, the player makes runs in between the lines, creating space to move opposition defenders out of position when England are in possession.

From a defensive standpoint the player's key responsibility is to deny space and time to the opposition's primary outlet in midfield. More often than not, you'll find the opposition's defensive midfielder as an integral cog in the operation and ensuring there are no easy passes into this area is one way to disrupt build-up. Man-marking, cover-shadowing, and blocking off passing lanes are crucial elements of their off-the-ball responsibilities.

When the attacking midfielder does get possession, they are protected by a double pivot which means they're able to engage in the overloads to support any attacks down the flanks through the half-spaces. The kind of movement these attacks require define the success rate of the attack and how easily they can leave players in the final third without worrying about being exposed behind.

Taking a closer look at ***Figure 32***, we see a hypothetical situation with England in possession. The team has transformed into a 4-2-3-1-like shape in this attack with the number ten in the right half-space.

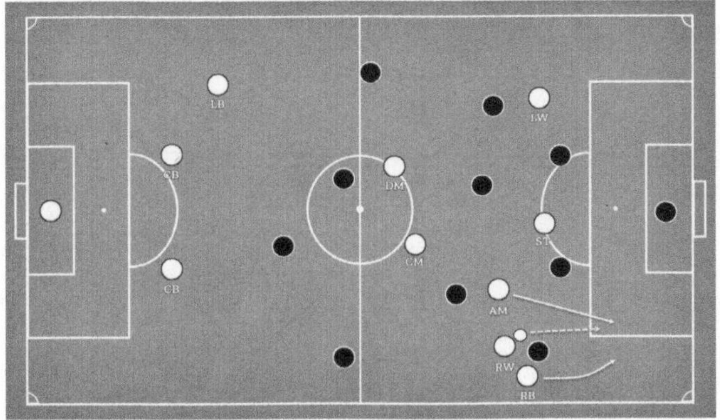

[Figure 32]

The right-winger in possession is faced up with the opposition full-back with the right-back overlapping. The attacking midfielder looks to make a diagonal run behind the full-back to open space for the central striker to drop into the highlighted space or receive a pass to change the angle of the cross.

It's important to mention that the attacking midfielder has been one of the more viable avenues in build-up when England have been pinned back. The way we saw Spain and Sweden disrupt England's build-up play forced them to have to adjust and adapt to a style that bypassed the way these opponents had been set up. However, during the interim Wiegman would instruct her attacking midfielder to drop much deeper than usual to become the free player to play a wall pass to. Though this job would be conducted by the defensive midfielder, teams would be and are

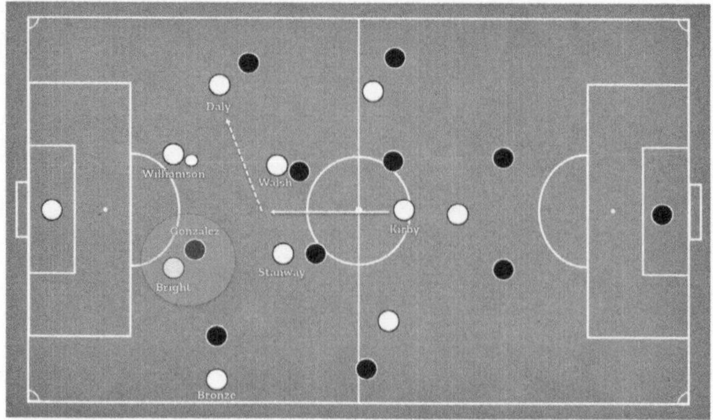

[Figure 33]

compelled to block that path. ***Figure 33*** is a passage of play from the quarter-final against Spain where Kirby dropped in between the Spanish central midfielders who were man-marking Walsh and Stanway. The centre-forward Esther González occupied one of the centre-backs which left Williamson with Kirby as her only option. Though it was a simple wall pass to left-back Rachel Daly, the move gave England momentum and created a path for England further forward given that a marker eventually opted to follow Kirby.

England have been blessed with not just one, but rather two electric attacking midfielders in Fran Kirby and Ella Toone. Each has their own qualities that contribute to the team in different ways but now the manager approaches a crossroads going into the World Cup: does Wiegman trust the proven veteran Kirby, who had seen the team through so many results thanks to her tireless efforts, or does she instead put faith in the up-and-coming future stars, chiefly Toone whose goal in the final galvanised the side to believe they could be the ones victorious that night? One of them has been plagued with injuries while the other is yet to establish her consistency as a starter across a tournament. This is the choice we will be examining in more detail in the following chapter.

Chapter 10

England's number tens – Fran Kirby and Ella Toone

ONE OF England's many positive facets is their strength in depth across the squad. Each position has quality options available to them, but none more so in terms of pure class than attacking midfield. Fran Kirby and Ella Toone are two of England's most talented players and while Kirby just reminded the world of her brilliance once again during the tournament, it was Toone who shone when the stakes were highest, under immense pressure. While playing cameo roles, she managed to score crucial goals – most importantly the opener in the final.

Sarina Wiegman's options here are impressive and playing a hybrid formation hasn't fazed either player. Both have the ability to be malleable and play deeper initial positions. When it comes down to it, Kirby represents the present but Toone represents the future – so heading into the World Cup, how does Wiegman please both players?

The answer is that she doesn't. Though Kirby is the first choice in the position, Toone has a chance to push her out and fight for a starting spot. Both players bring their own attributes to the table and in certain conditions, either becomes stronger than the other. However, what if it wasn't a matter of first or second choice?

Though we hear the old adage of getting to start based on form and playing to the opposition, this could be applicable here. Yes, Wiegman has a reputation for settling on a preferred starting XI, but going into the World Cup there will need to be an element of rotation and making changes based on who England face.

As a matter of fact, if just a few key chances had been put away and a couple of decisions went the other way for Spain or Sweden, we would be having a very different conversation. England overcame both teams well but they won't be afforded that luxury at the World Cup. Going through each player's core strengths and identifying where they excel will be key in understanding where and when Kirby and Toone should play.

Fran Kirby

'It often feels like England don't get the most out of Kirby's considerable skillset. That said, when given opportunities within the final third, more often than not Kirby is able to make a decisive impact in tight games.'

– Rob Pratley

The very fact that we were able to witness Kirby grace the green grass of stadiums across England was a fortuitous sight to behold. Their Euros victory was in no small part down to Kirby, whose attacking contributions were immeasurable. Wiegman's insistence on using Kirby despite missing chunks of her club season prior represented the high regard she had for her star player. After all, when you have the world's best attacking midfielder in your midst, then you give her every opportunity you can to make the biggest comeback of her career.

After having already suffered from pericarditis, a heart disease she put up with in 2019 that left her nine months out of the game, Kirby was then out for another extended period of time in February 2022, this time with a health problem that caused excessive fatigue which seemingly had no answer.

She had been out of the Chelsea squad for multiple game weeks before the announcement in April. In an interview with *The Guardian*, Kirby revealed that she visited many specialists but there were no obvious answers for a cure. Kirby is no stranger to setbacks, and even more so in coming back from them. From the depression arising from her mother's death in her early teens to pericarditis and this fatigue issue, it's safe to say Kirby was handed some of the roughest cards ever dealt.

But if there's anyone with the willpower, strength, and courage to fight back from every life obstacle, it's Kirby. The extent to which she fought back against this latest problem was profound. The initial diagnosis was 'underperformance fatigue syndrome' but pinpointing the right problem was difficult. Kirby worked with psychologists and specialists and even installed an oxygen tent in her house. In the same interview, she said that this wasn't a new issue, but rather one that had plagued her for five to six years and that she had managed to deal with it:

'So I've kind of learned now what the triggers are, when I start to feel a certain way, and how I can prevent that from happening … it's really important to listen to your body and when you need to take a break, you take a break and really benefit from it.'

The point is that Kirby's fightback wasn't just off the pitch, but on it too where she proved her fitness; to go from an impact sub (to manage her fitness) to an undroppable starter as England's number ten. This move not only kick-started Wiegman's attacking mechanisms into place, but it gave them another dimension. So what makes Kirby such a world-class performer?

What makes Kirby so pivotal for England is more than just style – it's her heightened intelligence and tenacity that makes her a special, one-of-a-kind player.

Kirby can be considered one of the best off-the-ball space investigators in football and knowing when to make runs to create space and find it to receive possession is arguably her greatest asset, alongside her goal contribution record. A lot of the work the number ten needs to undertake is assessing the game state and moving into the right positions. Given that England don't necessarily play with a traditional attacking midfielder, Kirby naturally starts from a deeper position as a left-sided central midfielder, after which the team's shape transforms into having a more orthodox number ten.

In seasons past she has traditionally been an attacking midfielder with a playmaker profile, occupying the number ten position, but she has also played as a striker. Kirby has been Chelsea's primary creative link player, supplying service for strikers through her ball carrying and intelligent passing. Despite Chelsea's switch to a 3-4-3 she has continued to be involved as an attacking force coming in off the right wing.

> *'She ends up sacrificing herself to drop deeper as the ball carrier to progress the team up the pitch rather than being the clinical incisive ten we are so used to at Chelsea.'*
>
> **– Rob Pratley**

What makes Kirby a different proposition when starting deeper is her ability to be closer to England's defensive half and therefore the ball. We know about the struggles the Lionesses had in their build-up towards the latter stages of the competition, and one of the methods they used to alleviate this problem was by dropping Kirby deeper to receive the ball. Kirby's favoured movement is making the run from her starting left-sided central midfield position towards the left half-space when play is built up on the left. We know that most of the build-up comes off the right, but at times when play is passed around in the final third and makes its way to the left, Kirby is the controlling figure there. On this left side, Kirby will identify the best position to receive the ball and carry it forward, knowing when to either lay it off and play a one-two exchange with Lauren Hemp or to play it back across the pitch to prolong the attacking move.

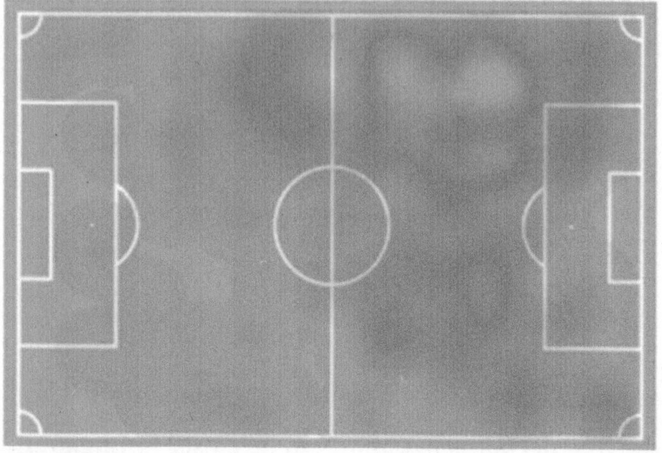

[Figure 34]

Figure 34 is Kirby's heat map from the Euros and what's most pertinent is her presence on the left flank. This area of the pitch is clearly where she's spent most of her time on or off the ball and it corroborates her typical movement patterns. Even when play is on the right she is constantly scanning the pitch, looking to find gaps to capitalise on to receive or make a run into the box to get on the end of a cut-back or late cross.

Though Hemp is very much an isolated figure against her full-back on the left, interchanging play with Kirby means that the midfielder gets involved in all phases of play.

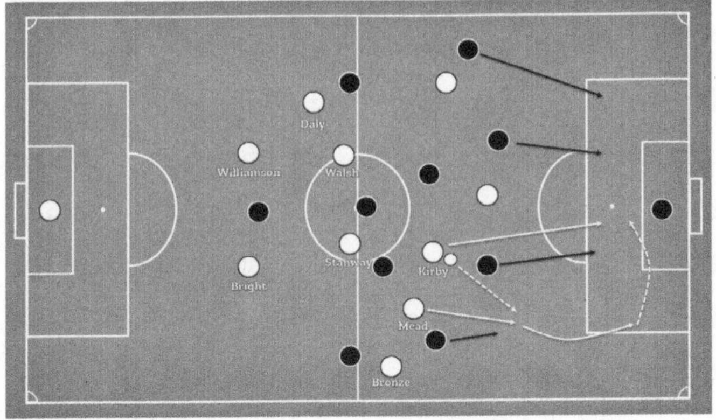

[Figure 35]

An example from a passage of play against Sweden is shown in ***Figure 35***. England were playing out from the back at a time when Sweden had started with very high intensity. Sweden's 4-4-1-1 was compact and tight centrally which meant finding space was harder. Kirby's first received pass was between the lines centrally, more of a number ten position where she found enough space to avoid the defensive midfielder's sight. She managed to quickly progress play by playing to Beth Mead on the right wing and as the pass went out, Sweden's line of defence and midfield was split and caused their players to go towards the area of play. A cross from Mead into the box simultaneously saw Kirby continue her run and take a position on the shoulder of the centre-back. Though the cross was intercepted, it was meant to land in Kirby's path which showed she identified the space and ran early.

A lot of these movements also become important in the counterattack. Given how good Kirby's decision-making is in knowing what action to take in these high-pressure situations, it makes or breaks the attacking move as a whole. A lot of her actions in these situations mean she can convert even the most tenuous chances into clear-cut ones. Though she may have registered a lower average of 1.51 dribbles per 90 at a sparse 28.57 per cent success rate, it does translate to the fact that Kirby was much more of a presence off the ball than on it. England's focus was primarily to create from the right and use off-ball movements on the left to balance the team. Kirby was a major instigator of that and these situations that she found herself in meant she was able to influence play more through excellent positioning.

The truth is that Kirby didn't need much of the ball to have an effect; rather her limited time with it was supplemented by other players making numerous channel runs and dangerous movements which meant all she needed to do was find them when she did have the ball. The rest of her time was spent finding spaces and gaps to exploit. As an example, let's take a look at

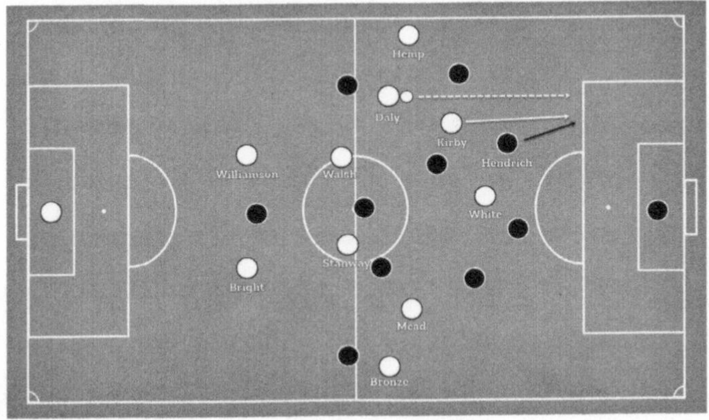

[Figure 36]

this counter-movement passage of a play during the final which I've shown in ***Figure 36***.

England clear their lines and get the ball up through to Walsh and are searching for ways into Germany's half before they track back and reset. Walsh's ball to Daly triggers Kirby to start making a run across the channel and use the vacant space. Daly sees the run and corresponding space and successfully attempts to play her next pass there. Kirby's timing is exceptional which leads her to a one-on-one against Kathrin Hendrich and she immediately then cuts back inside to quickly release a cross over to the on-rushing Ellen White. The resulting header was on target, but it was Kirby's run and decision to create space for the cross that converted the counterattack into a clear-cut opportunity.

Kirby is an extremely talented player and one who will probably be anchored to England's midfield for years to come. While she has this sort of influence and effect on the side, there is no denying her status as one of the world's best. However, England's need to look at the future for alternatives isn't an immediate requirement for now because in Ella Toone, they already have a long-term replacement in the offing. Does she have the ability to replace Kirby or is she a player who is entirely different to what England already has?

Ella Toone

'To compete for a spot in this England team against Fran Kirby is not for everyone … Ella "the supersub" Toone is already in the history books with her goal against Spain in the quarter-final with way more to come.'

– **Mia Eriksson**

'Tooooooooooooooooooonnnnneee'.

The bellowing sound of Ella Toone's name around every stadium was deafening and, quite frankly, intimidating. For every time Toone was summoned from the bench to affect a game during the Euros, there was a capacity home crowd waiting in anticipation to give their girl wonder her call to action. The shout was probably one of the highlights of my trip and even a dream to be a part of. Just like Joe Root of England's cricket team or Kelly Smith of Arsenal and England, Toone has become a cult hero for whom fans have developed a deep appreciation that has extended to more than just her eccentric personality and name.

Toone's journey to the senior England side came from nowhere. Playing for Manchester United in the second tier, she helped them gain promotion by scoring 14 goals but then followed it up with only a solitary goal in her first Women's Super League season. It wasn't the lack of goals but rather her desire to improve game after game and year after year that impressed her coaches.

Toone's interview with Asif Burhan of *Forbes* explains in great detail how she developed her game and the influences around her that make her the player she is now. In recent times, she credits learning from her ex-Manchester United team-mates, Tobin Heath and Christen Press.

'Well, I think my game is ultimately about getting in the pockets and finding space and getting on the half-turn. I think I did that well on my debut for England. I think with my club, that's something that I work on massively, and the likes of Tobin and Christen always help. They give me little bits of advice that will help me and I've learned a lot from them. So yeah, it's just about me keeping working hard and keep getting in those little pockets of space and trying to make things happen on the pitch.

'I like to get in the pockets in the games. Christen then plays in front of me in the "nine". She'll tell me when my body positioning can be more open. Sometimes when I'm not facing forward, she'll say "that's because your body position is not right" so just a little information like that really helps for me to improve my game. Then, when I'm opening up, I'm getting the ball to Christen as well, so it helps both of us.'

Kelly Smith is Toone's footballing idol and she models part of her game after the forward, but she also looks at a current Lionesses star as motivation – Fran Kirby. The comparisons between the two are inevitable but it still helps to learn from an England legend playing in a similar position, as Toone explains:

'I always talk about Fran Kirby, she's an unbelievable player. The stuff that she does on the ball, on the pitch, is brilliant. You look at her at Chelsea and she's flying. I watch her in training and I try to take little bits from her game and put it into mine. She's a great player and a great person as well, and someone I've learned a lot from in previous camps.'

Toone's performances for England have steadily improved from her debut in February 2021 and she is now very much a core part of the setup under Wiegman. If her cameo appearances are anything to go by, then there's a long career ahead for the Manchester United midfielder.

Toone has now become a recognisable name as her performances have created a compelling argument for her inclusion in the team from the start. There is no doubt that Toone is deserving of a starting role, but is it still too early? Have we seen enough from her on a consistent basis to warrant a starting place in that midfield three?

To get an answer we'll need to understand Toone's profile and explain her key attributes before we can compare the two attacking midfielders. In Toone, Wiegman has a player who brings a touch of aggressiveness combined with playmaking nous. Her vibrant and eccentric on-the-ball game is the perfect mix of tenacity, creativity, and goalscoring ability.

As a central attacking midfielder, Toone is a hybrid shadow striker and playmaking midfielder with an impressive sense of positioning. Simply put, she's able to play as a second striker that combines her impressive playmaking abilities to interchange between both roles when required. Her club manager Marc Skinner talked about Toone and echoes the sentiment after her performance in September 2021 against Leicester City:

'If you want wonderful footballers for our nation, you have to sometimes take the box off if they are as good as Ella can be.'

Toone's role under Wiegman is centred around maximising the spaces left between the lines as an impact substitute. I've mentioned before that Wiegman doesn't play with a natural number ten position, so it's as an attacking central midfielder that Toone takes up the task but the switch between a number ten and number eight is something she can do. The formation does shift slightly to a 4-2-3-1 more as the default system on the ball than it does when Kirby is in play. The protection from the double pivot means that Toone can play this more aggressive role without the fear of being exposed defensively, but it isn't a necessity for her to thrive.

Given the state of play and the inevitable tired legs out on the pitch, Toone can diligently find space to receive, turn, and look forward to threading the gaps. This comes as a result of her first touch and quick decision-making that is good enough to take her away from markers to find the right pass. This also makes her a press-resistant player, especially in congested areas against a low block. Subsequently, she'll make a run towards the box and look for spaces there as a striker would.

England essentially are allowed to play with two centre-forwards without taking away from their midfield. Toone's general movements when she comes on effectively see her confined to the left of the pitch without being limited to the area she covers on that side. What I mean by this is that she has the freedom to drop deep or make channel runs at will without underloading the left pitch and leaving no extra supporting body with Lauren Hemp. I've looked to depict her areas of movement in ***Figure 37***.

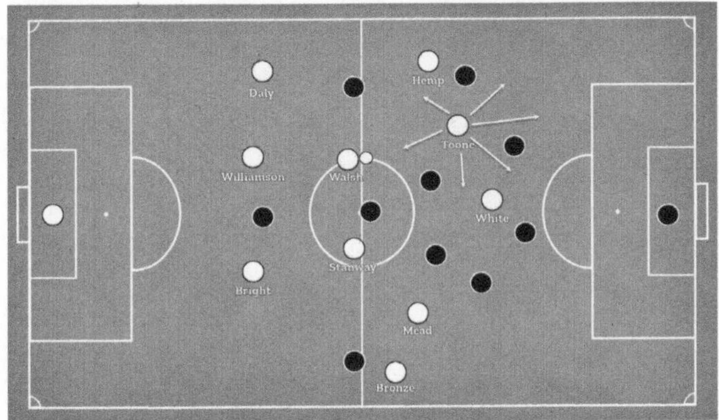

[Figure 37]

Analysing her heat map to a closer degree in ***Figure 38***, we can see that Toone isn't rooted in her central position; rather she's mobile and wants to roam across the final third. A lot of her movement is centred towards the left half-space, giving her the outlet to

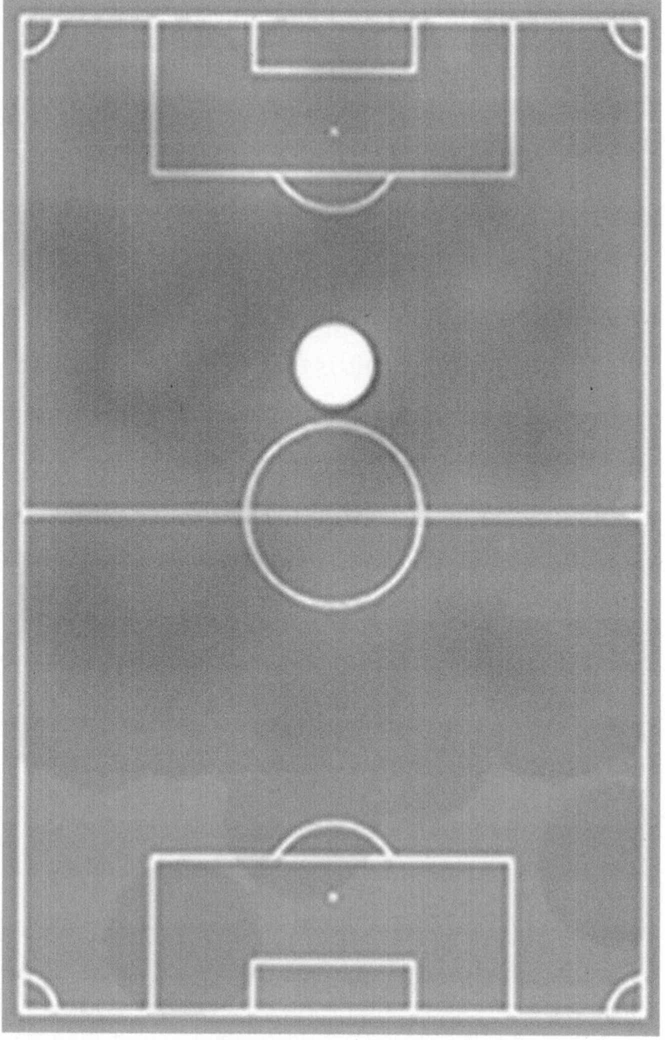

[Figure 38]

combine with Hemp and take up the faux left striker position. It also aligns with her taking up Kirby's role as the left-sided off-the-ball playmaker that is the basis of the position in the first place.

This skillset isn't widespread among the England hopefuls available and the way she has broken on to the scene through her performances for Manchester United has given Wiegman a selection headache. It will be interesting to see whether Wiegman persists with her 4-3-3 system or if she tinkers and starts to utilise the 4-2-3-1 or 4-4-2 variants as a standard. The constant interchange of formations in matches suggests that she ultimately isn't too worried about her starting shape but rather how they can react and reform under different situations.

There are, however, different uses of Toone's strengths across each system.

We know how important the central midfielders are to England's system and vice versa because of the tactical flexibility it requires. Switching from a number ten to a number six or number eight becomes a necessity and having the versatility to play across the three positions is important. Not every player will fill this criterion but having two of the three is essential. In Toone, you have a player who might naturally be an attacking midfielder but can still translate her skills to a more attacking number eight role.

Toone's skillset interchanges between the two positions and her main strength in both of them is her spatial awareness. This is arguably the most critical component of a midfielder's profile, where they're able to understand and find key spaces in between the midfield lines to then create even more relative time to execute the next action. At a glance, Toone doesn't seem very nimble-footed; however, when she receives the ball to her feet, she's able to quickly move away from her marker, whether it be with a quick switch of feet or taking a deliberate touch into space, allowing her to turn and move.

Take this example from England's group stage game against Northern Ireland in ***Figure 39***. It's a relatively simple move that displays a high degree of intuitiveness and vision. Toone's position is deeper in midfield and in this case, she is playing alongside Kirby late in the game. Walsh's pass to Toone comes about with the Manchester United midfielder asking for the ball to be played to her right foot from where she

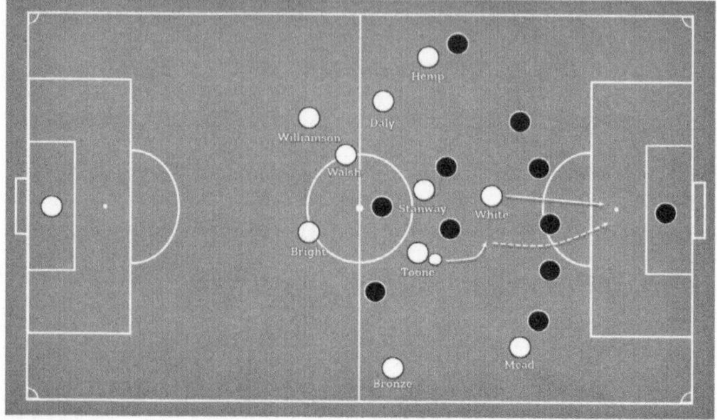

[Figure 39]

takes a touch to her left and goes around the Northern Ireland marker. From here, she threads an exquisite ball breaking the Irish back five for Mead to run on to.

There is no real complexity to the move; rather it's the culmination of receiving, turning, and executing the next action within a matter of seconds that shows quick thinking and decisiveness in choosing the right position and making the move to create more space to play the incisive pass.

Toone's ability to protect the ball and collect from deeper positions might be reminiscent of a deep-lying playmaker, but it's her dribbling and carrying ability that makes her such a distinctive profile.

She played 266 minutes across six matches during the European Championship, with the caveat that all her appearances were off the bench. Toone's playmaking numbers weren't too impressive given her role was more that of a finisher in her cameo appearances, but where her impact was truly felt was from a more attacking perspective. An average of 1.69 dribbles per 90 minutes with a 60 per cent success rate suggests Toone is very much on the ball frequently and is having a positive impact, albeit at a slightly lower rate.

However, what's more relevant is her numbers around offensive duels per 90 (6.77) and touches in the box (3.38). These underlying numbers imply she has been an extremely steady and reliable ball carrier who's constantly finding spaces in the final third and as a safe ball protector. This coincides with her press-resistance and profile of being a player who is good in tight spaces and able to find gaps between the lines.

Another example from the Northern Ireland game combines all the attributes I've talked about so far. Toone receives possession in a deeper position and facing towards the opposition's goal, rather than with her back to goal as was the case in the previous example. By getting the ball just as she makes the run, it gives her the momentum to push forward but given that there's a marker close by, she intelligently swivels, turns and uses a burst of acceleration to drive past the Irish players before unleashing a shot that goes wide.

As an off-ball player, Toone is much more aggressive Fran Kirby. Typically, she's come on alongside Alessia Russo and together they're both more mobile and agile players than Kirby and Ellen White are. Their ability to press defensive lines and prompt unforced (and forced) errors through misplaced passes or pouncing on lingering players taking too long to release the ball is key. We know about Wiegman's pressing structure prioritising a 4-4-2 shape ensuring the central spaces are blocked off before engaging in duels. The constant movement of Russo and Toone make this much more effective even if they aren't always able to win back possession.

The qualitative results of pressing are more relevant in the actual passage of play itself. What I mean is that you might not see high numbers of pressures or recoveries, but the act of pressing itself forces teams into unseen movements or decisions that cannot be defined by data – especially if you consider that both Toone and Russo played fewer than 300 minutes each.

Toone's never-ending will to pressure players and close them down will be a massive asset to Wiegman and is another added benefit that is arguably lacking in Kirby. Yes, Kirby makes up for it in her superior playmaking ability and intelligence on the pitch, but Toone's off-the-ball defensive work is a trait that is injected into every modern number ten and that is something Wiegman will appreciate and want.

Both Toone and Kirby bring differing profiles to the table and while you can make some direct comparisons, I don't believe it makes sense. There is no straight answer to the question of whether Toone deserves to start because even in the limited minutes we've seen her for England, there is enough reason to warrant a place.

'I think one of the most interesting things to look out for post-Euros will be the competition for places. We've seen Ella Toone perform brilliantly for club and then for country when given the chance.

'Will Wiegman want to find a place for her in the starting line-up? If so, where is that? Can her and Fran Kirby play together, or does it have to be one or the other? There are a lot of really good players competing for similar positions as this new generation starts to come through.'

– Ameé Ruszkai

After analysing their games and the effect they've had on this England team, it's safe to say that they are both deserving of starting roles in their own right. Assessing each match as it comes and starting the best possible candidate is still the way to go and heading into a World Cup with more versatile teams to face will mean that Wiegman will have to rely on more of her squad – more so than she did during the Euros.

The benefit of having two players embedded in the Wiegman system is of huge importance and the room for experimentation becomes greater in the build-up to the World Cup. England will need Kirby and Toone to be at their very best and how they've both been brought through the system suggests that Wiegman actively counts on both players to deliver – the present and future.

Chapter 11

Heir to the throne – is Alessia Russo England's new centre-forward?

'I remember Alessia as a young kid at Chelsea where she was direct, powerful and [playing college football in] America has only added to that and she's come back as a complete forward who can play across the forward line. She was pivotal coming on for England giving them a focal point to capitalise on the great work Ellen [White] did before her.'

– Willie Kirk

ONE OF the biggest storylines to come out of the post-Euros era was the retirement of both Jill Scott and Ellen White. It caught the nation by surprise and while people were sad over the venerated pair's retirement, the discussion over who would be

England's next centre-forward began. Manchester City striker White has been at the heart of the England team, spearheading performances as their main focal point under every manager since her debut in March 2010 against Austria. After starting every game and ultimately winning Euro 2022, White's decision to call time on her illustrious career was partly to allow the next generation of players to make their mark on this side ahead of the 2023 World Cup.

Everyone knew White's retirement was coming at some point, but even the most pessimistic of supporters would have assumed she would lead the line in Australia and New Zealand before hanging up her boots. Alas, this was not to be, but as was the case with Fran Kirby, White's successor has also already been identified in Manchester United striker Alessia Russo.

Though Russo showed much promise and potential before the Euros, the idea that she would become England's number nine so early wasn't on the cards. It wasn't until her impactful cameo appearances during that tournament that she proved she was ready to take on the role immediately. As such, with White retiring, England are now in a position to unleash their starlet and get her ready for the World Cup in 2023.

So who is Alessia Russo and how has she suddenly become the next in line? You'd be right in thinking that Bethany England would have a case to take up this position or even the seemingly left-field choice of Rachel Daly, but Russo brings the best of both players in one and for what Sarina Wiegman requires, she fits the bill.

My objective here isn't to make a statement that Russo will lead England to World Cup glory (though it isn't out of the question); rather it is to explain why she has the potential to become their leading forward, maybe even a more compatible fit than White. I won't be diving into every aspect of her game but I will highlight the main traits that make her a long-term fit for the role.

Russo is a modern centre-forward with hints of what you'd find in an old-school striker. Her role for club and country might differ slightly but her overall contributions are identical. Russo is more of a mobile target striker who wants to link play by dropping deep into pockets of space with her back to goal, as well as be a box threat. She expertly looks to seek positions between the lines and generate space in behind opposition defences before finding her way into the box. Russo plays a semi-fixed role where she has the freedom to find said pockets across the final third in the attack.

To further elaborate on her responsibilities, one of them includes facilitating build-up to connect the midfield and attack together, thus making it a seamless and cohesive transition. Russo becomes a reference point for the team to play through and generate running opportunities for the attacking players around her. On top of this, she's very much a pressing-focused striker off the ball in defensive situations. Teams now defend from the front and the striker is the first line of defence, something that Russo attempts to fulfil. While she might not intercept regularly or have a high recovery rate, she's able to apply pressure on opposing defences with her diligent running and work rate.

Regardless of formation, Russo has always played as a striker in a 4-4-2, 4-2-3-1, and 4-3-3. A pertinent feature of her game is the focus on her movement and how she drops into pockets of space like a false nine or deep-lying forward, but also holds up play like a target-striker before entering the box like a poacher. For Wiegman's system to work it needs her centre-forward to be an outlet, hold-up striker, and channel carrier all in one. The role requires extensive link-up and understanding between the forwards to create a cohesive attacking system. You look at the job White performed; a lot of her work was tied to constant movement and harassing defenders off the ball while being an outlet in the build-up phase. Though she was

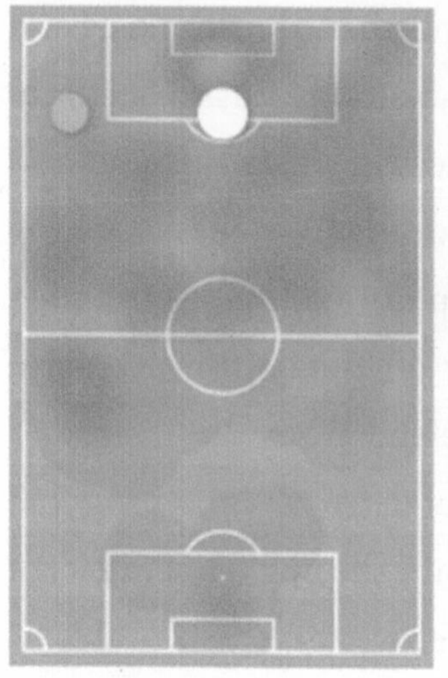

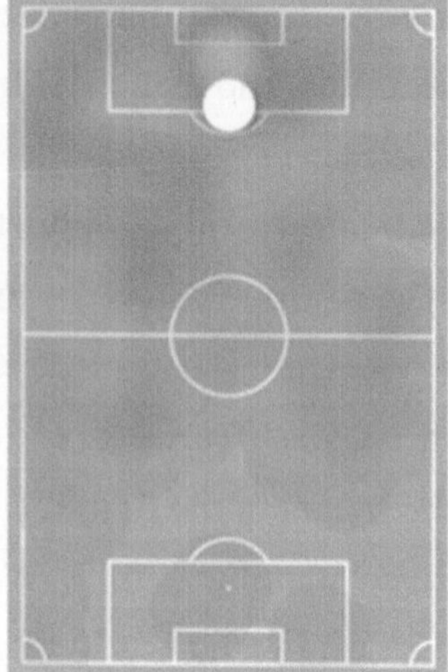

[Figure 40]

competent in this regard, White's true strengths lie in being a penalty box striker.

The heat maps in ***Figure 40*** compare White's and Russo's movement during the Euros. It's easy to notice that Russo made her way across the final third, going as deep as the halfway line. In comparison, White was much more dialled into the penalty area and spent most of her time there. Russo's varied and intense movement pattern indicates that she's not one-dimensional and instead of being a static presence for defenders to easily mark, she's mobile enough to both create a dialogue with the midfield and give athletic runners space in behind. It's allowed Ella Toone, Beth Mead, or Fran

Kirby to play a much more active off-the-ball role to find pockets of space in between the lines.

White's lower frequency of dribbles per 90 minutes (1.05) and lower progressive runs (0.26) were a clear indication that her priorities and strengths lay in wanting to find good positions in the box. Good movement is a necessity for an England striker to thrive, but good anticipation coupled with intelligent movement is even better.

It's in these pockets that Russo utilises her strength to shield the ball and turn defenders to cover the space in behind, created often of her own doing. This profile of striker opens up space and opportunities for other attacking players, especially with this deeper movement. This action takes players out of position which in turn creates opportunities for runners to go in behind and bring others into play. You can break down Russo's movement into two parts – the first is her deep-lying link-up ability and the second is her box movement and using the spaces smartly.

Figure 41 against Spain clearly highlights the quality of Russo's movement to create space for the winger. She drops into the right half-space a little deeper than usual to help Bronze as a target from the throw-in. The Spanish have overloaded England's right side to stop the threat of Beth Mead and Georgia

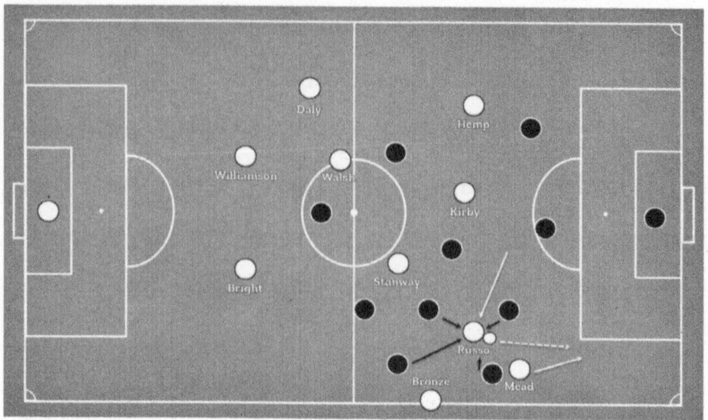

[Figure 41]

Stanway. By throwing herself there, Russo has attracted the attention of multiple Spanish defenders and through shielding the ball upon receiving it, she was able to control, turn, and play Mead down the flank into space to create a crossing opportunity.

In the final phase of the attacking sequence, movement and positioning in the box become of paramount importance. A striker usually needs a good understanding and movement inside the 18-yard box to thrive and succeed in their primary role, but for someone playing as England's striker, it becomes a core requirement. I believe Russo's intelligence in attacking situations is slightly underrated because of her unorthodox movement style.

When Russo moves across the pitch, she looks less mobile than she actually is. Her deceptive running means defenders had slightly underestimated her but have started to pay more attention to her. Because of this, Russo does not only turn and move in small spaces; her ability to find good positions from crosses and off the shoulders of defenders enables her to encounter goalscoring chances.

Russo averaged 3.99 touches in the box per 90 minutes at the Euros and although it doesn't rank in the top 30 (the 30th-placed average was 5.35), her numbers are nonetheless impressive given that she played fewer than 300 minutes during the tournament. In comparison, White averaged 6.80 touches in the box per 90 and started every game, playing 60 or more minutes each time. A higher touch value in the box means White was seeing the ball much more frequently and thus intelligently looking for smarter spaces to take up successfully. This is a trait that Russo will improve on over time, but the basic foundation is already there.

Russo's lower frequency of touches can also be attributed to most of her interchangeable play coming outside the box in the build-up as her chances were made from the wide areas, with fewer coming through the middle from through balls. When she does move into the box without the ball, she's always looking to make quick, acute moves to get ahead of her markers. Russo demonstrated as much in the semi-final where

England managed to break through Sweden's press. They used Keira Walsh to play forward towards Toone in the left half-space who took a lovely ball, swivelled, and then drove forward, and from there, Russo was already looking to run through the Swedish centre-backs. However, Toone used her club partner instinctively as a springboard to play a one-two passing exchange, and when she received it back again, she sprayed it out to the wide area for Mead to cross it. Russo was closely marked by Nathalie Björn but as the ball came in, she stepped away from Björn and quickly made a short, blind-sided run in front of the centre-back to get a powerful header off towards goal.

If we look back at the Euros, Russo didn't take a high volume of shots. In 293 minutes she registered ten shots with an expected goals (xG) return of 0.99. Her actual record was 1.23 goals per 90, which translated means she was extremely clinical with her attacking output, and that can only be put down to her intelligent positioning. A centre-forward isn't going to generate and get off high-quality opportunities without being in good positions and Russo's tournament return of four goals is a result of that. The low shot volume can be directly correlated to the significantly fewer minutes played and possibly the quality of chances created in the final third of matches, but the xG average mutes that point.

There is an appreciation of Russo's attacking style of play and how it's translated into Wiegman's system so far. Given that the formation can be versatile in its build-up, this brings Russo's finishing selection into the question.

While we've stressed the importance of the wingers in the system, creating through the middle is another added strength of this England side. Toone, Kirby, Mead, and Hemp are all excellent creators, and the unpredictability of England's supply point makes it hard for opposing teams to stop them, let alone deal with Russo's movement.

'On another Lauren Hemp cross, Laia Alexandri left Ella Toone to try and help her centre-backs deal with Russo and Bright. But Russo still won the aerial duel, leaving Irene Paredes – one of the game's best aerial defenders – on the ground. Toone ran, unmarked, on to the second ball to score the equalising goal. This play was a testament not only to Russo's physicality, but to Wiegman's decision-making.'

– Blair Newman

In this case, it makes Russo's finishing ability all the more threatening because of her dual aerial and ground-scoring skills, combined with her excellent positioning. In normal time England would use a combination of cut-backs, flat crosses, and through balls. This is an area that White excelled in. She was very good at reading the game frequently managing to choose the best shot and using her work rate to ensure she was there ahead of her marker to finish. Her 52 goals in 113 games make for good reading. With the wingers, it's especially unpredictable given that Hemp and Mead contrast in that one floats in between the wide areas and half-spaces to cross from an inside position or wide area while the other confines herself to the touchline. For Hemp, it's much more of an old-fashioned method of running down the wing, on the counterattack, and whipping in a menacing cross.

The next two examples are different types of goals Russo scored during the Euros. The first in ***Figure 42*** is against Northern Ireland, where she scored a headed goal. England's attack here is up against a low block with Northern Ireland playing with a back five crowding the box. The Lionesses interchange play between Toone, Mead, and Bronze before a set of quickfire passes sees Mead drive into enough space to launch a lofted cross into the six-yard box. Throughout

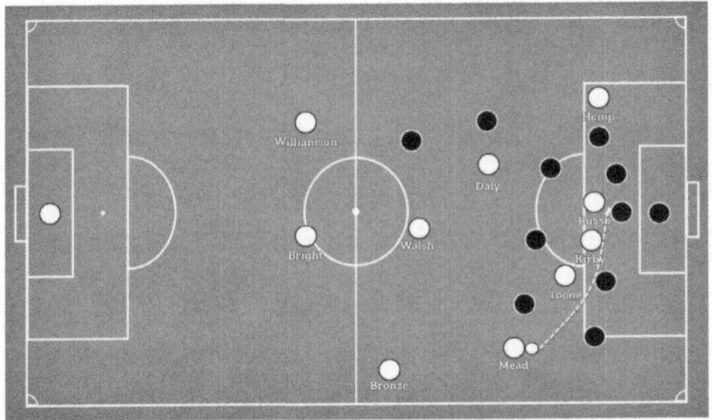

[Figure 42]

the sequence, Russo checks her shoulder and monitors the movement of her marker. As the ball comes in, she checks her movement and makes a quick shift forward to head the ball across goal.

The second type of goal Russo scored in the same game saw England try to break down the low block again with the back five not giving space away. Toone picked up possession in between the lines and looked to find Russo between three central defenders. The quality of the pass was sublime, but the way Russo received the pass, turned, and shot was representative of an experienced striker. Very few players have the ability to take a touch and turn away from a set of defenders in that manner.

There are other options available to Wiegman for the position – most notably Bethany England, Lauren James, and Ebony Salmon. I believe that Salmon can become an England regular given her nous for goalscoring and truly exceptional play off the shoulder of defenders. Though she is relatively new to the setup, there is a chance for the Houston Dash striker to prove her credentials to become England's first bench option.

Regardless, England have always had at least one experienced forward in the squad and with White retiring, that vacancy will seemingly be filled up by Chelsea's Bethany England. The forward has been a bit unlucky in my opinion. A couple of years ago she led the line and took Chelsea to the Women's Super League title, scoring 14 league goals, but was then surpassed to a first-team spot by Sam Kerr. White has been the Lionesses' preferred striker and England have been playing catch-up ever since. You'd think White's retirement would have meant a chance for England to lead the line and prove her worth, but Russo's timely rise has kept her on the fringes. What seems inevitable is England assuming the role of the experienced forward, being ready to be called upon off the bench to provide a different option and the new senior member of the dressing room.

James is seemingly an outside option in the near future given she is already under consideration for the wider roles, but playing her as a central striker isn't out of the question. She had made a good start to the

2022/23 season and a fit and firing James can only mean England would be unleashing the potential she showed at Manchester United. There she was utilised in a central role as well as the wider ones.

In Salmon and James, England have two of the brightest talents they could ask for so they arguably have the forward position locked down for several years. It's healthy competition and it gives Wiegman a lot of tactical flexibility to adjust her system across various games and tournaments to suit her needs. Each of these strikers is of differing profiles and knowing who to use and when gives England a variation they might have not had before.

The retirement of Ellen White might have been a blow in terms of losing an experienced figure and major dressing room influence; however, the timing of her decision came just when her successor has shown enough promise to take over the throne. Russo might still be a young striker but with the World Cup coming later in 2023, there's enough time to fully immerse the Manchester United striker into the crux of this team and structure.

Chapter 12

Mary Earps – underrated England revelation

'Earps experienced maybe the most difficult season of her career in the WSL in 2022. For her to move past that and be a consistently reliable, and at times extraordinary, backstop for England – that, that is one of the stories of the tournament.'

– Kieran Doyle

FOR ENGLAND, the goalkeeping department was one where they had a tough choice to make given the various options they had at their disposal. Sarina Wiegman had three top-class goalkeepers in her stable, each with a specific and unique skillset. Ahead of the European Championship she had to decide who was going to be the number one. Ellie Roebuck, Mary Earps, and Hannah Hampton all got a chance in the pre-Euro friendlies and each gave a good account of themselves but in reality, there was a clear winner going into the summer in Earps.

It wasn't always like this, given Earps's exile from the England setup for close to two years before Wiegman's appointment. September 2021 saw an unexpected call-up for Earps and she went on to impress the head coach enough to warrant a starting position at the Euros.

The Manchester United keeper had quickly become Wiegman's go-to option after Roebuck suffered an injury at the start of the 2021/22 season. From there the position was Earps's to lose, though it wasn't always clear-cut due to her indifferent club form in 2021/22. Earps ended up with the second-highest number of clean sheets – ten – behind Arsenal's Manuela Zinsberger and while it makes for good reading, her overall performance levels weren't really up to international standards and many observers were rightly sceptical.

One may have thought that she was the weak link in the England defence, but in the time between the end of the season and the start of the finals something changed and Earps's displays during the Euros were a level above the initial expectations. The England number one was by far the goalkeeper of the tournament and although her defensive line was objectively impenetrable, it was Earps's all-round displays that gave England the added protection when it mattered.

I'll be the first to admit that analysing a goalkeeper in a book is probably near impossible to do given the tactics board's inability to truly showcase a proper analysis of the individual between the posts. In essence, the true details come through in the minor movements, positioning, and saves when thoroughly examining that role, and that is something I cannot portray here. Nevertheless, I will expound on the reasons behind her rise and why she's likely to retain her status as England's number one for the foreseeable future.

England's aggregate score was 84 goals scored and three conceded from September 2021 until June 2022. Much can be said about the level of opposition during that period (North Macedonia, Luxembourg, and Latvia to name but three) but England have nonetheless shown a propensity to defend well, even more so when they have a dependable pair of hands behind them. An obvious pattern emerged as Earps was starting the majority of games, leaving Hampton and Roebuck an appearance each during the Arnold Clark Cup and beyond.

Keira Walsh. England's metronome and magician.

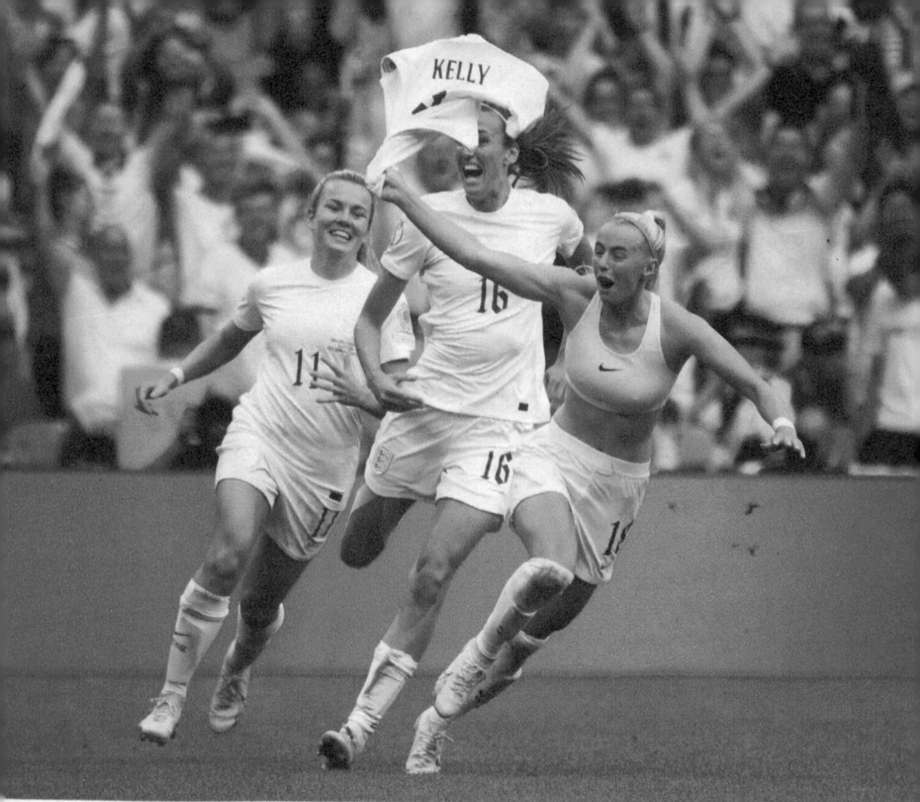

Chloe Kelly's iconic celebration after scoring the winning goal against Germany in the final at Wembley.

Fans celebrate England's victory following the UEFA Women's Euro 2022 Final.

The moment England lifted the trophy inside a sold-out Wembley stadium.

The record attendance is displayed inside the stadium at the final.

The moment of Alessia Russo's backheel goal against Sweden.

Ellen White addresses the crowd after the Lionesses' astonishing win against Sweden in the semi-final.

Mary Earps was the tournament's best goalkeeper and produced a series of outstanding displays for England.

Beth Mead and Rachel Daly pose with the trophy. Both players were influential in their positions, making vital contributions.

Sarina Wiegman made history by winning back-to-back Euro tournaments with two different nations on home soil.

Leah Williamson captained England to victory, putting in outstanding defensive performances throughout the tournament.

What we can deduce from these friendlies and the Euros is the importance that Wiegman places on building out from the back. Distribution is clearly a key component of 'Wiegman-ball', but this doesn't mean the more defensive aspects of goalkeeping aren't important. In fact, there is much more emphasis on the goalkeeper's long-range distribution than composure under pressure and short passing techniques. These are needed but Wiegman looks at stopping one-on-ones and crosses as clearly important core traits for her keeper. In essence, the overriding profile is geared towards all-round competence over being a specialist shot-stopper or ball player.

Earps's distribution was very much in line with this notion. She was playing shorter passes in normal goal kick situations, especially against teams that allowed England the build-up opportunity. However, she was noticeably playing longer goal kicks against high-pressing teams to bypass this. While quick release and starting counterattacking movements would be an aspect that Earps would be good at, it wasn't exactly part of the game plan, so her style of play during the Euros was more focused on other parts of goalkeeping than distribution. This will likely change in the 2023 World Cup when England take on teams that will look more to dominate the ball instead. This could alter England's approach to a more reactive, counterattacking one, which I believe they could play just as well too.

Earps has always been a brilliant shot-stopper. You'd often see her being very busy on her line and displaying great athleticism with reflex saves. I think we all knew Earps as a technically proficient stopper who made eccentric saves but she was also at times overzealous for Manchester United. That led her to concede more chances – more so the kind that she should have stopped if there was better positioning. The data from her club season shows as much with an expected conceded goals per 90 minutes figure of 0.89 as against conceded goals per 90 of 0.99, which means she let in more goals than the quality of chances that came towards her.

The Euros was the complete opposite experience, wherein every decision Earps made from a shot-stopping perspective pretty much paid off. I want to focus on her performance against Sweden in particular, where England were under the pump for the better part of 20 minutes with the opposition peppering shots from well-crafted chances. Many of the first few opportunities derived from passes in behind, leaving Earps in constant one-on-ones against their strikers. These situations are rather difficult to handle but

Earps's early positioning and movement to cover the frame of the goal were excellent and her reaction times were even better. This is especially the case in the early Sofia Jakobsson chance where she made a diagonal run in behind the centre-back on the left and got into a position to shoot from the left with the right side of the goal free. Earps made her body big and tried to cover her near post and thus managed to save down to her right with her outstretched left foot to deny the San Diego Wave winger.

Earps's saves against Stina Blackstenius and Jakobsson were, in my opinion, the sole reason England were able to win that semi-final. If either of those chances ha gone in then the tide would have turned in Sweden's favour given their period of dominance. For another example, take Earps's performance against Austria in England's first friendly post-Euros, which continued her excellent form. She had to make a reflex save from a rare Austria chance when the score was 1-0 and England went on to get their second goal a few minutes later. The comments made by Wiegman after the Austria game to Emma Sanders of BBC Sport were telling.

'Those two saves were difference-makers. It was 1-0 and she keeps the score at 1-0. That's so important. They were hard moments because she didn't have to do very much before – almost nothing – and it was really cold so she has to be concentrated.

'In the moment when there are these shots, she has to be concentrated and explosive in this action. She can make the difference and she did.'

This confidence in Earps not only translated to her precise shot-stopping but in other important aspects of her role as well such as set-piece command and control. This was going to be absolutely crucial given how many teams house world-class set-piece takers. The most standout trait here is Earps's commitment to catching or punching deliveries. I thought she might have been a bit shaky with these based on her club season, but the tournament saw a much more commanding Earps. She expertly pounced on loose balls and smothered them with aplomb.

The Euros gave us a good indication of who Wiegman saw as her long-term option in the position. Of course, there is scope for change before the World Cup with the possibility that a new contender could emerge from elsewhere, but Earps has now pretty much nailed the position as her own. Any preconceptions before have now been totally banished and Earps is elevated to world-class status. The 29-year-old's confidence will only grow which will benefit Manchester United and in turn England. She has become a vocal leader with strong, purposeful performances. Of course, having more options only means a more competitive squad overall but a settled goalkeeper and back line means there is undeniably more stability and longevity which ultimately means better defending.

Chapter 13

England's full-back conundrum

'There's a lot of strength in depth for England but one position that could be a problem for them moving forward is at left-back. Rachel Daly does a great job there considering she is not a defender and when the Lionesses play teams that they are expected to beat, where they dominate the ball, it's not an issue.'

– **Ameé Ruszkai**

SARINA WIEGMAN'S team is now objectively the best in Europe and winning the European Championship against a host of top nations like Spain, Sweden, and Germany only further backs this claim. However, Wiegman will be the first to say that her team needs to improve further. If anything, we saw a couple of tactical deficiencies that put England on the back foot several times during the tournament and if it weren't for the tweaks and changes from Wiegman and her coaching staff, the Lionesses might not have been crowned champions. The World Cup in Australia and New Zealand starts in July 2023 and it represents the next major tournament coming up, with a quick turnaround. This means Wiegman only has a finite amount of time to iron out the creases and improve on what is an already substantial base.

What I want to explore and outline in this chapter and the next are the tactical issues that originated from the performances at the Euros and highlight those problems in a little more detail. If we can understand these, then it makes proposing a potential solution much more straightforward.

For all of England's exploits through winning the Euros, there was still, in my opinion, one extensive issue: the full-backs. That both Lucy Bronze and Rachel Daly had successful tournaments and contributed to the tactical successes in attacking and defending is undeniable. However, teams recognised the obvious weaknesses they both possessed – not just in their profiles but in the system itself.

The second was England's problems with an opposition high press and as a result, building out from the back. Teams realised that once they cut off the supply in certain areas of the pitch, England needed to improvise and it took a relatively considerable amount of time for the adjustments to come into effect. I covered this extensively throughout the chapters on Spain and Sweden along with the modifications Wiegman made to come up with a solution to this.

There was also a third point that can be questioned about England: are physicality and power an undervalued problem for them? Some of the more physically imposing midfielders and strikers have caused England some trouble, most notably Stina Blackstenius and Sydney Lohmann. The next chapter takes a slightly more elevated look at whether this is something to seriously think about for the World Cup.

What I want to do here though is break down the systematic and player dilemmas around the full-back position. The proposed solutions will be addressed in a later chapter, taking both this problem and the pressing matter into account.

Before we really delve into the intricacies of this first part, I think it's worth talking about the roles and displays the two English full-backs have put in. Both players excelled in their roles and while teams did find ways to overturn them, they managed to contribute in ways that allowed them to still be important pieces of the puzzle.

Bronze is an excellent full-back and has been one of England's most consistent performers for the better part of a decade. While she might not be the player she was a couple of years ago – when she was crowned UEFA Women's Player of the Year for 2018/19, the first defender to claim the award, as well as the Best FIFA Women's Player in 2020 – Bronze is still one of the top full-backs in Europe. Let's remind ourselves of Bronze's profile as a player and why she's so important to England and Barcelona.

Bronze's role as a right-back is quite unique. Full-backs are expected to carry out both attacking and defensive duties, given the demands of managers and how modern tactics have played out in recent times. A traditional, attack-minded full-back, Bronze can tirelessly take on both an attacking and defensive role, such is the nature of her playing style. What makes her truly unique is her dual role of an inverted and traditional full-back.

Bronze's greatest traits derive from her positional intelligence, spatial awareness, and role interchangeability, all of which contribute to her attacking and defensive positioning. Her passing, dribbling, and speed are three core traits that constitute her attacking endeavours while her tackling and tactical intelligence are part of her defensive repertoire.

Her speed might be declining, but it's the combination of all these attributes that still makes Bronze a top-class full-back today.

Her counterpart Daly is a versatile and positional enigma; a player who has excelled as a centre-forward for her club side, yet she is persistently utilised as a full-back for her country. From the days of Phil Neville, Daly was filling in at full-back and somehow has convinced both of her national team managers to continue playing her there. Wiegman's insistence on Daly as a left-back raised questions again, but her displays at the Euros showed the full spectrum of why she should or shouldn't play there. Who is Daly and why has she been selected to play left-back?

Daly is a natural centre-forward that excels in deep-lying play and linking up with the midfield before finding herself in the box. She has transformed herself into a multi-faceted player who has made the full-back position her second home, making her transition between the two roles easy. She made her name at Houston Dash but moved to Aston Villa in the summer of 2022 to be closer to home and has continued playing as a striker there. This sort of versatility enables osmosis of her attributes so she can perform in her position as a left-back. She operates as a hybrid, advanced deep-lying forward which fits into the system by her dropping into the pockets, creating space with exceptional tactical intelligence.

Daly takes the requisite traits from her striker role into her role as a full-back. Her good positioning, attacking intelligence, and link-up play are essential ingredients that integrate seamlessly into the team's style. We know how effective Daly is going forward where she has the positional awareness to take up the sufficient inside or wide positions to play an inverted attacking role. However, defensively, she has improved with time and experience. Her defensive positioning and interceptions stand out as her most improved traits, but it's her speed that brings her the most joy, meaning she can keep up with most wingers. This also becomes a huge advantage if England are counterattacked because she can track back at speed. Another underrated ability of Daly's game is her size. She is a massive presence and has become a very useful attacking and defensive body in set-piece situations. It just so happens that Wiegman's system suits Daly's style of play.

In short, the way Wiegman wants her full-backs to play requires them to operate in contrasting styles. We know that Wiegman's build-up is associated with the right side and using Bronze as a primary outlet in the build-up and supporting body going forward means the left-back needs to bring balance to the equation. In doing so, it obliges Daly to keep the shape and continue England's 3-2 defensive structure.

> *'I was surprised more teams didn't look at what Austria did in the first game of the Euros, how they got at England with their pressing, and use it as a blueprint to try and beat them.*
>
> *'It'll be interesting to see how that goes after the Euros, as England face more international teams with different styles and different strengths in the build-up to that World Cup.*
>
> *'Maybe it'll improve how the Lionesses deal with that high energy press, or maybe it'll lead to some tweaks in the style of play to try and avoid being put under pressure like that.'*
>
> **– Ameé Ruszkai**

You might think that using Daly in a more defensive fashion is a waste, although she is afforded some room to push forward into the half-space region to provide support to Lauren Hemp and be a passing and crossing outlet if the situation arises. We've seen Daly maraud forward when England have been dominant, adding extra dynamism to the attack. Bronze, on the other hand, is much more of an active presence in the middle and final thirds. You'd have noticed the copious amounts of time Bronze was galloping down the right flank in support of Beth Mead either on the overlap or underlap, being an extra passing outlet or creating off-ball runs to open up space for the other attacking players on the right side to create.

This brings us to the crux of the issue – space behind the full-backs. On the face of it, England seem to dominate in most facets from ball possession to box defending. Other teams found it hard to counterattack or counterpress England because of how well drilled they were in their system. In some regard, the issue I'm discussing in this chapter intertwines with the build-up issue because it's the opposition pressing them that manufactures the potentially lethal space in behind.

In the Lionesses' 4-3-3/4-3-2-1 hybrid system, the way the team builds out means there are more bodies pushed forward in overloading the final third, but it doesn't take into account the potential danger of a team counterattacking in an efficient manner. One of the biggest problems we saw during the Euros was that no matter how effective and dominant England were in an attacking sense, if a team won back possession and adequately found their wide attackers, there was space to be had – particularly behind Bronze.

Wiegman wants her right-back to be the primary progressor while the left-back needs to be a defensive supporting body, keeping the disciplined off-the-ball shape and structure with the odd attacking foray. While it makes sense for Bronze to take up the progressive role (albeit with her showing slight signs of slowing down), the use of Daly as the defensive holding figure is nonetheless slightly baffling. I understand the need and want for a pacy full-back to make covering runs, but a more natural option who is more suited to a purely defensive role in either Alex Greenwood or Demi Stokes might have worked better, and it would put less pressure on Bronze positionally when she's taking the ball high up the pitch.

Teams have tried pressing England very high up the pitch and failed but what they adapted to doing

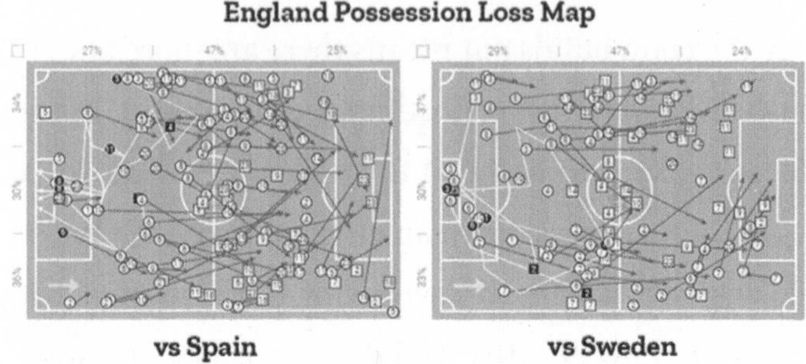

[Figure 43]

instead was looking to dispossess them in the central regions. This is when their build-up pattern is taking form and the movements from the central midfielders and wide attackers are starting to take shape. ***Figure 43*** is a graphic of two possession loss maps from England's games against Spain (left) and Sweden (right) which clearly points toward their losses coming from midfield. In each game, they lost the ball a staggering 47 per cent there. When England reach this part of the pitch it's usually when the full-backs have stepped up and an efficient counterattacking team gets their wingers into good attacking positions.

Let's take this passage of play from England's match against Sweden in ***Figure 44***. As I documented in the chapter on Sweden, the opposition were extremely diligent in the first 15 minutes and pressed England well. This moment occurred in the seventh

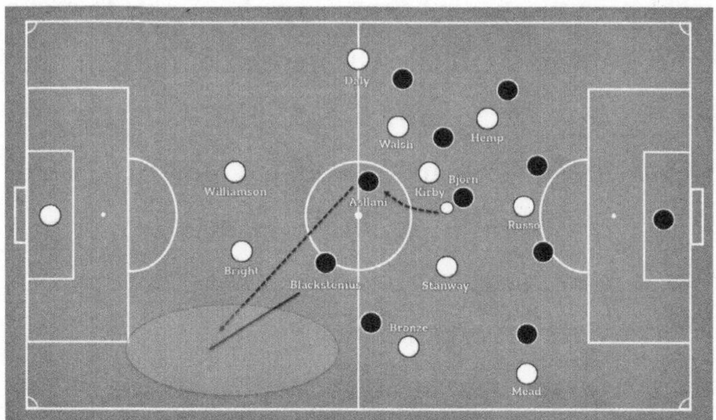

[Figure 44]

minute when Sweden regained possession by taking the ball off Hemp and with Nathalie Björn winning a 50-50 duel against Fran Kirby to put Sweden in a good counterattacking position. At the point at which Kosovare Asllani receives the ball, notice England's structure: Bronze is much higher up the pitch, as are Keira Walsh, Georgia Stanway, Kirby, and to some extent, Daly. Asllani recognises the space available and plays a very quick through ball towards the onrushing Stina Blackstenius, who runs into the space vacated by Bronze. The end result is an excellent save by Mary Earps, but this theme occurred time and time again – especially in the latter stages of the tournament.

It isn't about Bronze's inept positional awareness; rather her speed just isn't as it was in the past and adjusting her position to suit her style now should be a priority. However, the way Wiegman uses her right-back means that Bronze has to be able to move up and down the flank with precision. Don't get me wrong, Bronze did have her positive moments that were courtesy of her intelligence but moving forward, teams will start focusing on this aspect much more if this isn't addressed.

If Bronze was exploited due to her high positioning, then Daly was taken advantage of through her one-on-one defending. Daly performed well in most games where England had more possession because her off-the-ball positioning in static situations was quite good. This isn't to say that she wasn't able to fluidly move into good positions otherwise, but if there is one point to make about Daly it's that her ability to anticipate and be in good defensive positions is where she is probably lacking the most.

We talked about Bronze being the progressive outlet, but Daly's role seemed to be much more revolved around off-the-ball structure and shape to protect England from counterattacks and provide numerical superiority in the middle and final third. Let's take Spain, who focused on really attacking down the flanks to expose the wide defenders' positioning. While they did get some joy from Bronze's advanced movement, they specifically targeted England's left side. Both Marta Cardona and later Athenea del Castillo are direct wingers who thrive in one-on-one duels against their full-backs. Intelligent, quick, and unpredictable, both players caused Daly to track back and stay in her defensive third more often than not.

There were two instances against Spain where Daly lost her one-on-one duels against the wingers. These were significant because it was during the point in the game when Spain started to dominate proceedings. The first duel shown in ***Figure 45*** is the one that gave

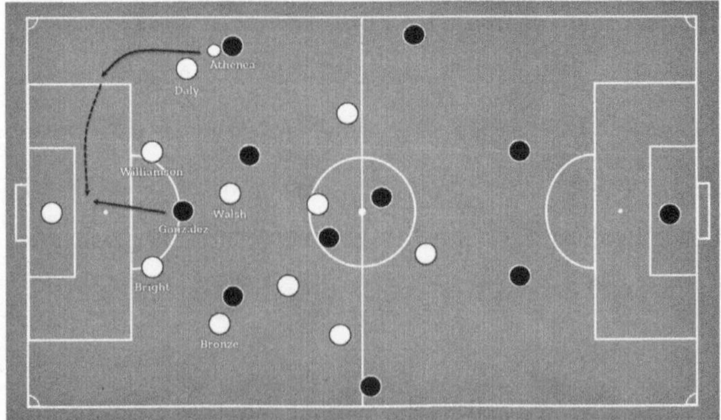

[Figure 45]

away the first goal. The Spanish were playing around England's midfield and defensive line, passing it between their midfield lines. After moving it to the right, Spain managed to get possession to del Castillo on the right in a one-on-one against Daly. Here, the Real Madrid winger took advantage of Daly's non-committal movement towards the ball and player; Daly then got tight to del Castillo but didn't commit to the tackle which allowed the winger to take it past her. The cross to Esther González resulted in the opening goal of the game.

The other moment came ten minutes after the first instance with England still on the back foot and play was once again shifted to Spain's right flank. From there, del Castillo picked up the ball slightly deeper than her earlier position and Daly moved into a better starting position to deal with the duel. However, del

Castillo's trickery and body positioning to drive inside and eventually glide to the touchline forced Daly to nibble at the winger. This created havoc and she not only nutmegged Daly, but floored her in the process. This passage of play forced Wiegman to make a change and bring on Alex Greenwood to add more solidity to the back line.

I'd still argue that Daly's inclusion at left-back has been a positive move overall. Before the tournament, many thought this 20-minute sequence would have been replicated regularly. However, while the system protected Daly's positioning, it didn't account for her taking on players in one-on-ones without adequate protection. I think there's more England can do to utilise her strengths going forward by possibly switching the build-up mechanics to the left and having Bronze stay slightly deeper. Daly's attacking potential and use as a false winger can give England yet another source of creativity.

Both defenders are critical to the running of the team and system, yet they're also slightly exposed by that very system. Daly and Bronze are currently two of England's best full-backs, but there are names in the Women's Super League who could carry out the role of the full-backs better. Going into the World Cup, teams with a wing-focused system will surely look to take advantage of this situation if it isn't adequately rectified by then. I would have been very intrigued to have seen France take on England, given the deadly form of Delphine Cascarino and Kadidiatou Diani and how England's full-back duo would have taken them on. This match-up could very well be made at the World Cup, not to mention plenty of other teams that focus their attacking tactics around their wide players. Wiegman will do well to resolve this both structurally and personnel-wise.

Chapter 14

Is physicality an issue?

'Whenever the Bayern Munich woman was introduced over the tournament, she added the je ne sais quoi that Germany were lacking. So, of course, during the final it was Lohmann who so many fans of Die Nationalelf were calling for.'

– Sophie Lawson

ONCE ENGLAND scored the winning goal through Chloe Kelly in the Euros final, they managed the rest of the game extremely diligently. The heightened level of game awareness with ten minutes to go in extra time was a marvel to watch – not exactly in terms of aesthetic entertainment, but in the sheer determination to keep the ball. But before this, Germany took one last throw of the dice to attempt a coup against the eventual champions.

As the final went into extra time, England toiled away after a late comeback from Germany through a Lina Magull goal in the last ten minutes of the 90. A tactical switch by Martina Voss-Tecklenburg by bringing on Sydney Lohmann gave the Germans a new dimension and yet another obstacle for the Lionesses to think about.

This wasn't necessarily a persistent issue that has plagued them like the full-back or build-up problems England had, but enough questions were still raised on how they would be able to counteract the presence of this particular profile of opposition player: when Stina Blackstenius and Lohmann used their strength both on and off the ball to both create space and be a threat on crosses for their respective teams. Swedish striker Blackstenius's impact has already been measured and explained in the chapter on Sweden, so here instead, I will focus on Lohmann.

In my opinion, Germany's biggest mistake was in the starting 11 once Alexandra Popp was removed. What the Wolfsburg striker brought to this team was physicality and, most importantly, a reference point up top. Every team prior to the final failed to cope with a player who could bully multiple defenders simultaneously and Popp's ability to attract centre-backs and release the inside-forwards plus the midfield runner Magull worked like a charm. It wasn't just in the build-up; she was also a massive threat on crosses and set pieces.

The loss of Popp's all-round play was detrimental to Germany and replicating it directly was a task nigh-on impossible. However, Lohmann proved to be one of the surprising stars of the tournament in her cameos. If she had been in from the start then I genuinely feel Wiegman would have been required to sound out yet another tactical adjustment, creating enough doubt for us about what could have been the end result.

In Germany's 4-3-3, Lohmann was used as an aggressive, attacking, box-to-box central midfielder playing in between the lines alongside Magull. The two were pushed forward to add numerical superiority but also to get Lohmann closer to the box to add the focal point missing with Popp's absence. Coming in from further back, Lohmann would pick up possession from deeper areas and carry the ball forward before laying it off to find spaces in the final third. Once she received possession again, her burst of pace would be too difficult for defences to cope with because of a mixture of fatigue and power. Lohmann's ability to be physically aggressive coupled with smart passes meant teams had to adjust.

The change seemed to work against England's 4-3-3 hybrid system because the double pivot was pegged back at the edge of their own box, forcing the Lionesses to narrow their defensive line which opened up the flanks for Giulia Gwinn, Tabea Waßmuth, and Svenja Huth to create. Germany were able to use Lohmann in an almost free role to drive between the lines, wide areas, and the box itself. England's defence found it hard to pick up the Bayern midfielder, almost giving away a couple of chances as a result.

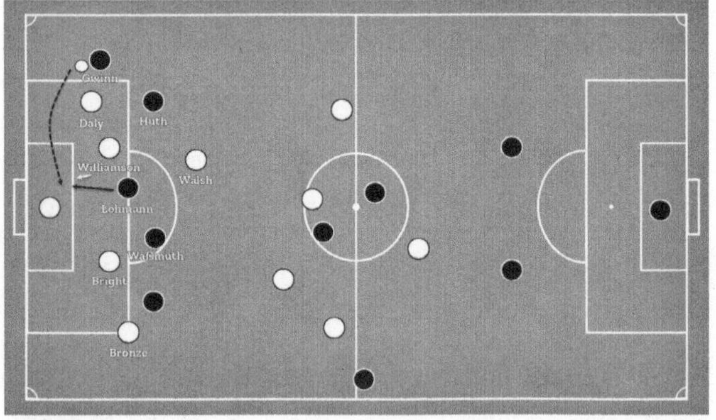

[Figure 46]

In ***Figure 46*** you see an example from extra time where a crossing opportunity is narrowly missed. The constant movement from Germany's midfield forced England to sit back and eventually had the ball move out to Gwinn on the right flank. After a quick exchange of passes, Gwinn found a crossing chance and whipped in a dangerous cross for a late Lohmann run. This run caught Millie Bright and Leah Williamson off guard and were it not for Bright's presence putting off the midfielder, England might have conceded yet again.

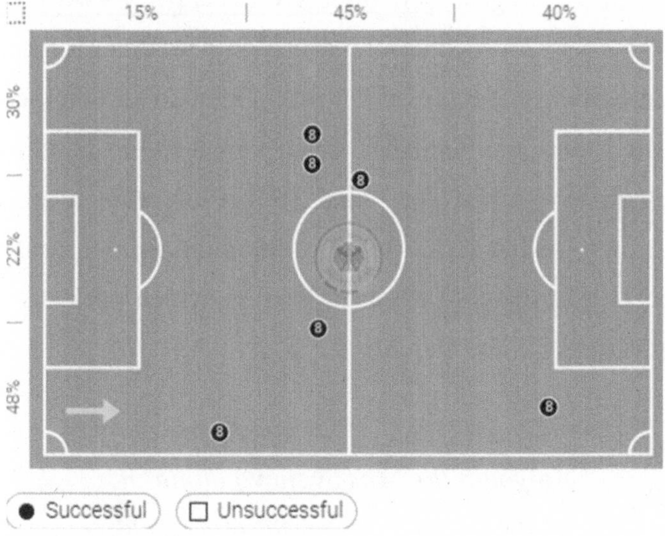

[Figure 47]

What England couldn't cope with was the constant pressure applied by the Bayern midfielder in the box, requiring both centre-backs to be pinned closer to the penalty area and six-yard box, thus creating a narrower defensive line which gave the Germans the wide areas to cross and numbers in the middle. In ***Figure 47*** Lohmann's offensive duels map from the Euros emphasises how her activity is spread all across the pitch.

She wasn't confined to one area but instead was given the freedom to roam. Interestingly, she was engaged in six offensive duels and won all of them in her cameo.

She averaged 10.37 offensive duels per 90 with a 58.82 per cent success rate, which only further ratifies her status as an aggressive number eight. To explain the importance Lohmann had to Germany's and England's chances, I asked journalist Sophie Lawson, who's known for her rather unconventional opinions, and received this quite eloquent passage which perfectly summed the German up:

> *'Unpredictable, underused, and oh-so-good, this was Sydney Lohmann at the Euros. For as criminally good as Germany were through the group stage of the 2022 Euros, the eight-time champions had to adapt to the knockout stages. This is arguably where Martina Voss-Tecklenburg excelled as each match became do or die … but the biggest complaint of the coach? How long she took to change things up.*
>
> *'When talking about her supersubs – specifically those who were underutilised over July – Lohmann is the obvious name. It was Lohmann who would use her fresh legs to run at England and wantonly*

punish where her team-mates could not. And it was indeed Lohmann who revitalised an ailing Germany at Wembley but her introduction was all too late, her cameo memorable but enough to leave the question of "what if?" to hang in the air if she'd been brought into the match earlier or, dare I say, have started.

'For England's historic win this summer, there are endless factors to consider but for the 73 minutes Lohmann was sat on the bench in Wembley, the Lionesses were far safer.'

– Sophie Lawson

So it begs the question of whether England can cope with this profile of player again in the future. They were generally adequate in taming the fiery legend Ada Hegerberg, but the likes of Stina Blackstenius, Esther González, and Sydney Lohmann all caused enough problems to plant a seed of doubt. Their mix of aggressive movement, astute positioning, and added tactical dimension is something Wiegman will need to address going into the World Cup. Take a team like the United States as an example, who are structurally built from an infusion of pace and power. In their squad is aggressive midfielder Lindsey Horan, who is the perfect combination of elegant passing and raw running power with excellent movement; not to mention the pace of someone like Sophia Smith could be a devastating combination in tandem. There are destined to be more players of this ilk to face at the World Cup and finding a long-term solution to this potential problem is surely what Wiegman will have on the agenda.

Chapter 15

Alternative systems – would the 3-4-3 improve England defensively?

THE 2022 Euros saw a diverse range of tactical systems – not just from the starting formations, but in the mid-game adjustments when teams were being compromised. England were worthy users of their system, where they constantly looked to make incremental and minor changes to it amid periods of pressure and uncertainty. For example, France relied on focused wide play to compete while Germany focused on their target striker, Alexandra Popp. What was most prevalent though was that no team made any fundamental wholesale changes.

The truth is that the international scene isn't the place to carry out detailed and complex tactical concepts simply because of the limited time spent on the training pitch. Simpler styles and tactics translate better and give players an easier time absorbing the information. Nonetheless, the best international tacticians can differentiate nuanced tactical concepts and player strengths. What I mean by this is recognising what the majority of the team commonly plays week in and week out and utilising those ideas as part of your own tactical plan.

We've so far discussed the Lionesses' impressive performances but also highlighted the concerns. Sarina Wiegman has devised a truly nuanced and thorough plan with technical complexities articulated simply in a manner that has truly changed this team. She can be considered one of the best tacticians in women's football today, especially on the international stage. Her ability to do the basics well makes her so good and gives players the freedom to perform without being bogged down by heavy specific instructions. But despite all this, what would England look like under a different shape with a few structural changes?

In this chapter, I want to propose an alternative system that retains the core fundamental mechanisms and solves the full-back and build-up issues. This theoretical system could be one Wiegman administers at the World Cup. It's purely a hypothetical exercise, but one I feel is worth looking into.

The system – 3-4-3

The success with the current 4-2-3-1 and 4-3-3 hybrid should mean that there's only a need for minor changes and collectively perfecting the system. However, as I've been discussing throughout the book, there is still room to improve and adjust against different systems that penetrate certain weaknesses. England supposedly had multiple plans of action including a three-at-the-back formation we saw a glimpse of against Spain which led to the equalising goal. Of course, that was more to do with the pressure they were facing and numbers going forward than any real tactical breakthrough, but it worked. I wanted to use that 3-4-3 as the basis of my theory and see how England could further profit from this as a starting formation rather than as a late tactical change.

On paper, the 3-4-3 system is one that doesn't exactly fit England's squad. It would mean they would have to leave out one of Fran Kirby, Beth Mead, or Lauren Hemp. However, it got me thinking about the possibilities of what the system does to fix some of the build-up and full-back problems. Losing out on one of the attacking players might be a sacrifice but using this formation would mean England are adjusting their system to exploit their opposition and dropping one of their star attackers would be necessary collateral.

I truly believe the front three are good enough to still create clear-cut chances and having their pace and combination play will be enough, so it's at the back and midfield where it becomes most pertinent to answer. It's largely how you would expect a 3-4-3 to look, but the real story is in the details. However, where it shines is in its application of personnel in different positions and roles. At the time of writing in mid-September 2022, we haven't seen these propositions enacted in their fullest form yet, but this may change by the time you read this.

Wiegman and England would be well suited to resume using such a system because of the profiles of players available. If the insistence – and rightfully so – to pursue having a front three of Lauren Hemp, Alessia Russo, and Beth Mead carries on into the future, then leveraging the strengths of the other players will be vital. What's more important is ensuring that England are protected against certain pressing and attacking tactics that have left them short. I won't be expanding on every aspect of this system in great detail; rather I will be focusing on explaining where it alleviates the pain points.

Let's get the basics right. This 3-4-3 will not be a departure from what England are used to playing. Play will still be focused on the wing-backs and wide players with the central spine orchestrating the on-the-ball and off-the-ball movements of the team. Off the ball, retaining the active and proactive pressing structure from the front remains vital as it allows the team to push forward a few yards. The forwards will continue to be vital to the attacking third with the left side in isolation and the right side in overload. This is the system that wants to create transitions through controlled midfield pressing, winning the ball back, and playing through the half-spaces, all of which are vital to its success, and something that England can adopt to good effect.

The fundamental principles of this system allow a team to have defensive solidity while having more of a counterattacking element. Between having an extra central defender and attack-minded wing-backs, the formation can mask deficiencies that may run through them and stop teams from exploiting them.

Defence – protecting the press and wing-backs

Many of the problems were exposed by Spain, Sweden, and Germany. England's full-backs were targeted and the high man-marking pressing scheme limited their usual build-up. Spain were able to block Leah Williamson's path to both Keira Walsh and Lucy Bronze. The Spanish full-backs had stepped up to ensure that Bronze was pressurised enough to have to either return the pass or attempt a carry. They essentially hit two birds with one stone in limiting England's build-up by squeezing the supply to both of their key ball progressors. How do you solve such a dilemma? Well, you make changes, of course.

Switching from a back four to a back three would take some adjustment but given how the majority of the defensive contingent have played in back threes for their clubs already makes it easier. In such a system the wing-backs are the proprietary benefactors given the licence they have to attack alongside the added protection of the third centre-back and double pivot. England's biggest flaw is the positioning of their full-backs and while they are effective at both ends of the pitch, it's in transition that they get hurt. Nonetheless, it is the addition of a third central defender that enables

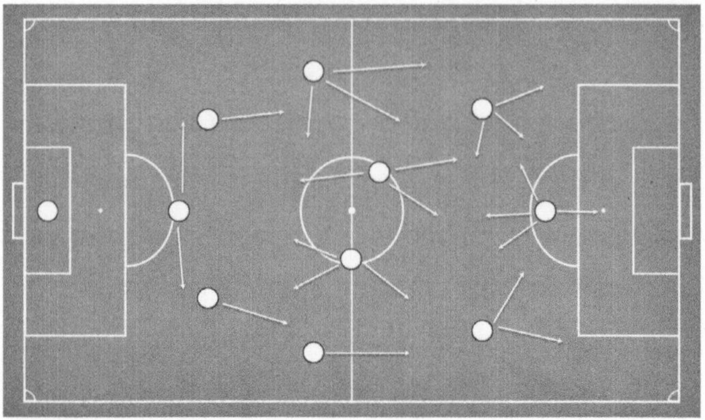

[Figure 48]

them to become free from being overloaded and have a ready outlet available to them.

In ***Figure 48*** I have illustrated the general positions and areas these players will cover. Having three central defenders creates an advantage of numbers in the build-up. The spare centre-back can push forward and bypass the man-marking and pull other players out of position. When teams use their front three to pressure the centre-back and two full-backs, the on-ball defender is left with either the long ball option or carrying it through midfield since the deepest-lying midfielder is often also marked. Spain did this to perfection for more than an hour and allowed Williamson the chance to push forward while marking Walsh and the full-backs. It left the Arsenal defender with the choice to either go long to the wingers or attempt to carry it into midfield where Spain could sit in an organised fashion to block off any advances from there or use their central midfielders to press.

Using a back three, I would look for the wide centre-backs to control the build-up and use the defensive half-spaces as a source of pushing forward. The numerical advantage it gives enables England to have potentially two spare players in the possession phase and negate the press. Having a way to deal with the high press through extra supporting players means there's enough superiority to play their way out through passing exchanges and forcing deeper players to come forward and leave spaces in behind. ***Figure 49*** is an example of how a generic passage of play would take shape based on this explanation.

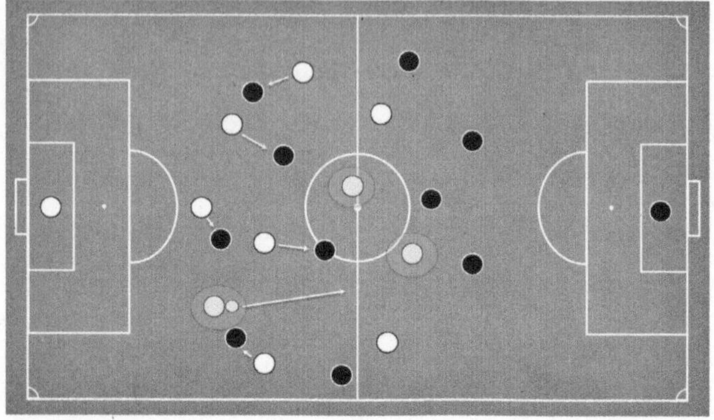

[Figure 49]

An added element is how this system also allows the wing-backs to have a higher starting position. By pushing one of the wing-backs higher up, there is space for the ball-sided centre-back to use the inside midfielders or the wing-back as the next passing outlet. England's build-up structure is to focus play through Bronze and ensure the ball finds its way towards Mead with the help of the inside midfielders. Through this, there is a way to continue the same pathways but also have an extra body in support. The added bonus is that a quicker defender can cover the wider centre-backs, allowing them more ball carrying.

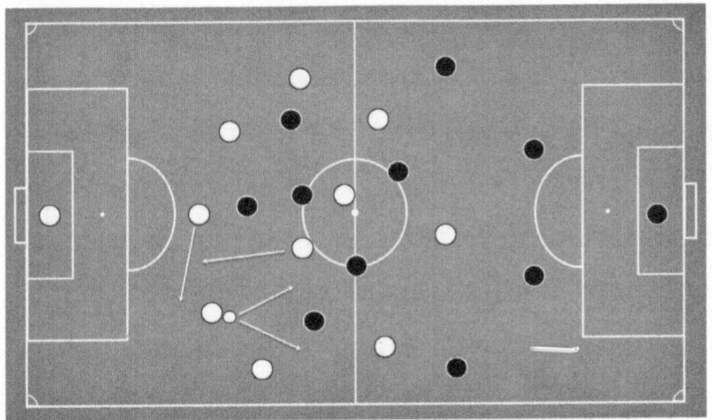

[Figure 50]

Figure 50 shows the general build-up pathway and structure that England would take under this sort of system and also how the centre-back can cover in behind. The biggest concern is to not leave any unnecessary space in behind and having a covering central defender who is particularly intelligent in covering – like Millie Bright – will allow Williamson, Bronze, or Alex Greenwood the space to progress without fear of leaving acres of space in behind. As a by-product, the number six can ghost between the back line and midfield, depending on the phase and position of play, to add more numbers to the back line for added protection when needed.

Balance and creativity – the tempo controllers and inverted wing-backs

When you construct a midfield in a 3-4-3 you have to look at the overall balance of the side. Finding the right profiles of midfielders becomes extremely important, not only for the double pivot but the number ten/second striker. If a team decides to use a 3-4-3, it becomes imperative that the double pivot can fulfil various roles, from dictating play to defensive screening. Both players should be adept at either covering the other or being versatile enough to carry out both roles. You look at Aitana Bonmatí and Patri Guijarro or Grace Geyoro and Sandie Toletti; these combinations are the crux of the side to enable the other players. For France, it allows the wide players to flourish while for Spain it allows Alexia Putellas to work in a much more advanced role with Bonmatí and Guijarro alternating positions and creating a solid base for her to attack.

Similarly, England have a stable core of Keira Walsh, Georgia Stanway, and Fran Kirby in the 4-3-3 but if we're to use this 3-4-3, then one of them is likely to be sacrificed to accommodate the forward line. The preliminary idea of having a two in midfield is to accommodate and improve the creativity from the back line while having a more structured and definitive baseline. Additionally, you can have one of the wing-backs come inside to form an extra body in midfield playing in a very inverted defensive midfield/wing-back role. More on this point later.

There are different scenarios in which England can line up but the idea behind my concept is to have a double pivot that doubles up as a defensive screen and attacking source. Being a defensive anchor is obvious but what I mean by attacking source is the ability to start attacks in both general build-up and counterattacking situations. The transition game becomes vital because of the speed at which England need to use the wing-backs and forwards. If the midfielder isn't a proficient passer or intelligent in possession, it becomes much more difficult for the control and transition game to be enforced. Being press-resistant and bypassing any pressing players in the vicinity leaves more space to operate in behind the opposition attacking midfield line.

Let's look at a potential situation in ***Figure 51*** where England would be winning possession back deep in

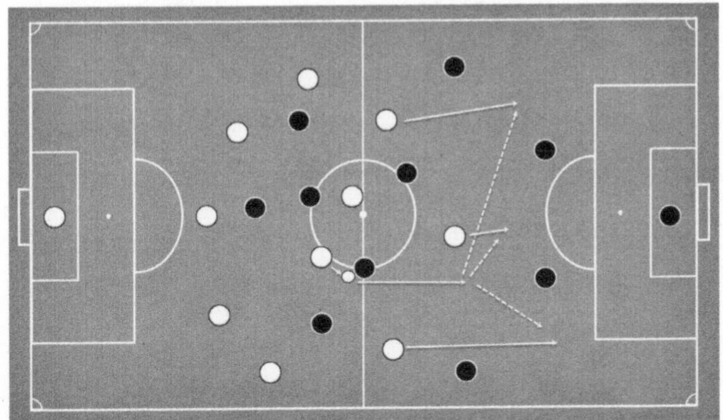

[Figure 51]

their half after enticing the opposition to push forward and look to exploit the space in the middle and final thirds. Given how England have pace and power in the forward areas in Russo, Mead, and Hemp, it comes down to the defensive midfielders to pick up possession to either play a diagonal cross to the wide areas or a direct, ground pass towards Russo to hold up the ball before turning and bringing the wide players in. The wing-backs are naturally pace-filled and will play on the over/underlap.

This now leads us to the point that is sprinkled throughout the chapter about the inverted wing-backs/defensive midfield hybrid role again. How will these wing-backs play in such a system? Due to the movement of the front three, the wing-backs become a needed source of creativity and width and therefore very important going forward and in transition. The current setup under Wiegman is to use Bronze as an attacking outlet down the right while Rachel Daly is much more pragmatic and cautious, at least in the first phase of play, staying a bit more inverted.

In this iteration of the 3-4-3 we're relying upon wing-backs but rather than radically changing the profile of players, we can repurpose them. This setup retains one wing-back as the attacking outlet who looks to combine with the winger and find different angles to cross or cutbacks. On the other side, it becomes much more about playing a supportive role by adapting their positioning from an attacking wing-back in possession when the ball is moved to that side, to being a baseline defensive midfielder to shore up the central areas in times of defensive transition. Think João Cancelo of Manchester City, who has mastered the art of playing as an inverted wing-back where he's seen creating from the left half-space but also defending alongside Rodri. As a result, they'll need the double pivot to cover and rotate into those vacant spaces, especially the side that pushes up a lot more. This will mainly occur in the off-ball possession phase where they need to cover the opposition winger trying to attack the space.

If you have players who can screen, position, press, and anticipate well, then it becomes much simpler to create a solid mid-block and transition. The double pivot might not be the most proficient tacklers or interceptors, but they will defend through sharp positioning and in numbers. England will maintain at the very least a 3-2 or 4-2 defensive structure to compensate for the lack of a true enforcer in midfield. The wing-back coming inside to provide support helps alleviate some of the defensive burdens from any midfielder who decides to push forward with the attack at that moment. An element of positional awareness and rotation is necessary.

When faced with the opposition in possession in midfield, it's less about having the ball but rather ensuring that they themselves aren't caught too deep in their own half. You want them to create an impenetrable midfield block before embarking on a man-to-man press without being over-adventurous. This makes it much harder for teams to play quick, incisive passes through their midfield.

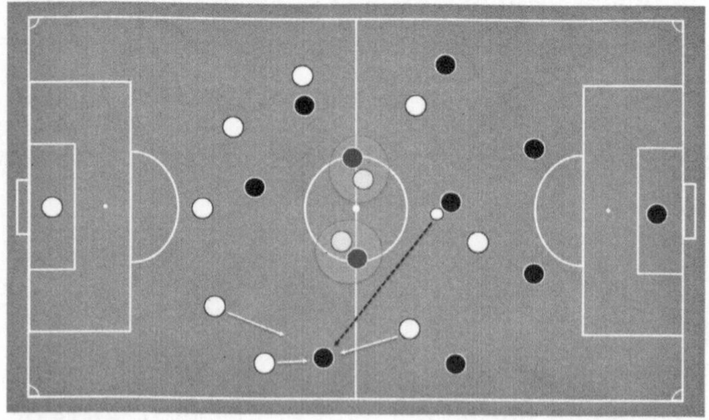

[Figure 52]

In ***Figure 52*** I have outlined an example of the type of situation I'm referring to. Based on the opposition playing a 4-3-3, you have their central midfielders trying to play between the double pivot but their positioning to block the passing lanes from the number six forces the midfielder to go wide and permit England to shift focus and move the team to the ball side. The midfield double pivot becomes an extension of the way the team presses just further behind. Additionally, this structure also brings them good rest defence. The concept is to provide cover when the forwards and attacking midfielders are pressing and this is what will contribute towards good rest defence. If England are caught slightly out of position or higher up the pitch, the presence of the defensive midfielder(s) in front of the centre-backs stops, if not delays the attack. At present, England do not possess the type of profile that could play a destroyer-type role but that isn't necessary because of the aforementioned defensive reasons. N'Golo Kante and Erin Cuthbert are two examples of versatile central midfielders who are both creative progressors and efficient ball-winners that England could benefit from.

As a whole, this theory only covers England from a defensive aspect and while I haven't touched on their attacking tendencies that can be derived from this system, I believe it was important to really explain how this can prevent the problems they've suffered so far. Protecting the full-backs and bypassing the press was the main cause for concern and I would hope that the proposed 3-4-3 will bring a balance to the squad, especially in big games that require a bit more tactical thought and complexity. I'll now delve into the potential starting XI and options along with the squad I feel should go to the World Cup.

Chapter 16

The squad – who should go to Australia and New Zealand?

BRIEFLY LOOKING back at the current England squad, it has various profiles that Sarina Wiegman will rely on. Given that there are a couple of retirements and question marks over some members of the group, I believe there is a real chance for the fringe and new players to enter the fray. The players are experienced, malleable, and fluid with versatility that can prove vital when it comes to adapting to any system. In ***Figure 53*** I have outlined the squad with the starting XI and the potential depth options. For the most part, the squad should retain most of the talent from the summer of 2022 but the retirements of Ellen White and Jill Scott guarantee at least two changes.

[Figure 53]

Goalkeepers: Mary Earps (Manchester United), Hannah Hampton (Aston Villa), Ellie Roebuck (Manchester City)

Defenders: Millie Bright (Chelsea), Lucy Bronze (Manchester City), Jess Carter (Chelsea), Rachel Daly

(Aston Villa), Alex Greenwood (Manchester City), *Maya Le Tissier (Manchester United)*, Lotte Wubben-Moy (Arsenal), Leah Williamson (Arsenal)

Midfielders: Fran Kirby (Chelsea), *Katie Zelem (Manchester United)*, Georgia Stanway (Bayern Munich), Ella Toone (Manchester United), Keira Walsh (Barcelona)

Forwards: Bethany England (Chelsea), Lauren Hemp (Manchester City), Chloe Kelly (Manchester City), Beth Mead (Arsenal), *Nikita Parris (Manchester United)/Lauren James (Chelsea)/Jess Park (Everton on loan from Manchester City)*, Alessia Russo (Manchester United), Ebony Salmon (Houston Dash)

Let's break this squad down and look at what would be the evident changes. Starting from the back, the goalkeepers remain the same. I don't predict there to be any monumental changes with Ellie Roebuck and Mary Earps continuing to fight it out for the number one spot. The only possible difference I can predict is with the third goalkeeper. Aston Villa invested heavily in their squad in the 2022 summer transfer window which lifted expectations for them and Hannah Hampton. If she has performed admirably through the season then her place is assured; any real dips in form coupled with an upturn of another English goalkeeper could see a new entrant in the spot instead.

Once again, the defence should largely remain the same. The foundation of any world-class team comes from a consistent back line with players who are adaptable and able to step in seamlessly. The back four of Rachel Daly, Leah Williamson, Millie Bright, and Lucy Bronze should continue to be Wiegman's preferred back four, though there are chances for Alex Greenwood to break into the team. The Manchester City central defender offers proficient ball-playing ability and intricate passing out from the back, all while being left-footed. Her quality highlights the significant strength in depth England have in defence. Jess Carter brings versatility and Lotte Wubben-Moy is an able deputy and one of England's most exciting prospects. The tournament could be too soon for the Arsenal centre-back but she is still one who will surely explode on to the scene in the near future.

The only major change would be Maya Le Tissier for Demi Stokes. The Manchester United defender has had an excellent start to the season and a move up to United from Brighton & Hove Albion last summer prompted her to take her performance levels up a notch. Le Tissier is a natural full-back capable of playing on both sides, and also as a centre-back. There's a theme of versatility in this squad and Le Tissier is no different. Her debut was marked with two goals and a clean sheet from centre-back rather than full-back, which makes her a perfect player for England. I believe her displays will be enough to tempt Wiegman to put her on the plane to Australia and New Zealand in 2023.

Moving into midfield, the usual suspects are present but Scott's retirement has left space for one new entrant, and in my opinion, this slot should go to Katie Zelem. The Manchester United captain has been an ever-present and consistent figure at club level and is becoming a more than useful option as a number six. While Keira Walsh and Georgia Stanway continue to be England's first-choice pairing, Zelem represents a real rotation option for Walsh as she plays an iteration of her football. Meanwhile, Stanway's all-action role will continue to be a much-needed balance in a midfield of two more creative and tempo-controlling profiles.

Ella Toone and Fran Kirby are England's third midfielder options playing as hybrid number eights and number tens. Their performances over the summer showed they are perfectly interchangeable with their own unique skillsets, as was expanded on earlier in the book.

Lastly, the forward area is probably where we might see most of the disturbances. Lauren Hemp, Chloe Kelly, and Beth Mead represent the present and future of the wide areas. Nikita Parris has been on a downward spiral for 18 months and will need a solid season with United to keep her place. I've highlighted the three players who could be competing for one spot on the plane. Parris's place is predicated on how well she performs and it will also be affected by the form of Lauren James and Jess Park. Chelsea forward James has shown flashes of brilliance so far, bringing a completely different profile to the table. Another potential surprise option could be Park. The on-loan Everton midfielder could be an explosive option off the bench should England need one. She gave a good account of herself up against Magdalena Eriksson in Everton's home game against Chelsea in October. The battle for the extra winger spot will be intense and whoever makes it will bring a valuable skillset to the squad.

However, unlike the wingers, it's in the centre-forward position where we're likely to see new faces. Alessia Russo seems a natural White replacement and Bethany England now takes the mantle of the experienced forward, but that third striker spot remains open. My feeling is that Ebony Salmon will get more chances to show her quality and will have a good enough season to warrant a seat on the plane. Her poacher-like qualities will be an asset against high-line defences and more minutes for Houston Dash under Juan Carlos Amorós should make her more well-rounded.

In summary, the squad keeps its core personnel with a few new fringe members added in to retain its winning environment while adding in some necessary fresh faces and ideas to the group. Can this group win the World Cup? Quite possibly, but it's about consistency and maintaining the high standards set. We know what the potential pitfalls are and how other teams can take advantage of them, yet there is real strength and confidence in England that can help them beat any team on their day.

Now to continue on to my theoretical proposition as was outlined in the previous chapter.

Proposed squad

Knowing what we want from this England team will bring an application to this theoretical system I proposed. Coming up with a preferred 11 was relatively straightforward for the most part but choosing players in certain positions was less so. I had to take into account the required profiles for certain roles and how that would affect other players around them. Some players have merely moved positions rather than having new players fitted in.

[Figure 54]

In ***Figure 54*** I have illustrated my theoretical starting XI posed in a 3-4-3 system. While some positions and roles are obvious fits, there are some that require more explanation so we'll elaborate here on certain positions and why they're the logical choice. Overall, you don't see too many names you aren't used to; it's their roles that have changed.

Lucy Bronze

Starting with the back three, I decided to use Lucy Bronze as my right-sided, wide central defender. The Barcelona full-back is one of the most intelligent defenders in world football and given her age and injury history, there is going to be a time when Bronze's runs down the flank will come to an end.

Moving Bronze to a centre-back role as part of a back three could be the next step in her England career. In possession, it provides England with a capable progressive playmaker without the risk of being left exposed positionally. Bronze's skillset includes progressive ball carrying, passing range, and excellent decision-making, which makes her the perfect defender. With the ball, Bronze can step into spaces and force teams to press out of shape and disrupt their movement patterns.

At Olympique Lyonnais she played as an inverted full-back out of possession that created a double pivot in midfield, and she can carry out something similar with extra reinforcements when the right wing-back forays forward.

Though Bronze is spatially aware we saw that once she lost possession in midfield, she would at times lose out to her opposition on pace. By carrying out a similar progressive role from right centre-back, she will now have the protection of her central centre-back and right wing-back as well as the defensive midfielder.

Rachel Daly

Moving Rachel Daly from left-back to right wing-back might not be the change everyone was thinking of but if we're expecting Daly to continue in defence, then I'd rather have her on the right. In one sense this could be a monumental shift given she'd be playing on her natural side where the build-up originates from. The idea is to give Daly the attacking freedom that Bronze was afforded in the 4-3-3 and while I would allow Bronze to continue as the progressive centre-back, this also enables Daly to play a more attacking role in a system that encourages some level of counterattacking and possession. If England are building out from the back, she's able to position herself in and around the right-winger and act like a forward, putting in crosses or running into the box.

Defensively, she has the pace to track back and doesn't need to be entirely worried about being positionally out of place – because even if she is a step too far, Bronze's positional awareness and the number six's presence should be enough to protect the vacant right wide space.

'Daly can be a real asset at full-back with her attacking qualities. But it is quite an ask to get her to switch to that position every time she is on international duty, when she's training, playing and excelling as a forward day-in, day-out for her club. Also, we saw in the Euros how top-class wingers can exploit that area – look at Athenea del Castillo's performance in the quarter-finals. But, other than Demi Stokes, who has fallen behind Leila Ouahabi in the pecking order at Manchester City, there are not many options for England here at all.'

– Ameé Ruszkai

Maya Le Tissier

For the system, Maya Le Tissier could be the perfect wing-back to complement the rest of the defence and assume the role of the inverted wing-back.

Le Tissier's playing style is very much that of a diligent, supportive full-back. As a centre-back she is able to combine positional awareness, ball-carrying, and an acute defensive skillset to complete a wide defending role. The ability to progress, attack, and defend when required makes her fit in the back line much more effectively. In this 3-4-3, England need a wing-back who can play both an inverted role defensively as well as provide a supporting figure when going forward.

Le Tissier's ability to play as a centre-back is crucial as this versatility means she can slot into a central position and defend as a false number six, creating a double pivot which enables Georgia Stanway to push in certain attacking situations. Alternatively, she can stay wider and defend one-on-ones against the wingers or tuck inside to close off any penetrative passes through the defensive line. Le Tissier ranked fourth in the WSL in 2021/22 for interceptions per 90 minutes and first for total interceptions which indicates her excellent spatial awareness and ability to cover defensive spaces.

Her attacking prowess will be the perfect foil to Lauren Hemp, who will drive in between the lines to create isolated duels. Having Le Tissier in support can give Hemp the much-needed protection in behind and provide an over- or under-lapping option in attack. Similar to the role Daly played, the addition of being able to play a more natural defensive role means the team can afford to use both wing-backs in more natural attacking and defensive roles.

Georgia Stanway

We all know that Georgia Stanway has built a reputation for picking up a yellow card in every game she plays – if anything, the card has become synonymous with the Bayern midfielder.

However, if she can harness her defensive game and enhance her discipline further, Stanway can become a real force as a defensive midfielder. She has the ability and skillset to become a tenacious defensive midfielder who patrols the deeper midfield areas, protecting the back three. The beauty of this system is that it also allows Stanway to push forward in attacking transitions given the cover around her. If a team is pressuring England, Stanway can play a bit more defensively but if she manages to win possession back, she can initiate a counterattack and use her progressive carrying ability to take the ball into the forward line.

She enables her midfield partner Walsh to play her natural game of dictating the tempo and play riskier passes into her given that she is also a press-resistant player. Stanway is liable to the odd rash tackle but playing her in such a vital position could possibly help accelerate her defensive discipline and offer England a dynamic double pivot in defending and attacking transitions.

* * *

This starting XI has a good mix of experience, youth, and – most importantly – cohesion between the thirds. The midfield to me will seem more balanced and less inclined to want to step into each third's space and there is now a complementary quality when Stanway joins in the attack. The positional rotations in certain positions are another important factor. The abilities of Bronze, Le Tissier, Daly, Stanway, and Kirby to seamlessly slot into different positions and continue the phase of play will make them very unpredictable to their opponents and offer them alternative defensive options as well as attacking ones. The World Cup brings teams with a range of tactical varieties and having a solid alternative option becomes imperative for England to have drilled into the vernacular. Wiegman will need to be even more switched on than she was at the Euros to succeed.

Chapter 17

A hope restored

THERE ARE many moments in history that you can recall and pinpoint the exact turning point for a team's fortunes. Arguably the first can be Sarina Wiegman's appointment and subsequent start to the job in September 2021. That was the first rite of passage but what followed was truly a remarkable odyssey of trust, development, and unbridled hope. The moment Leah Williamson lifted that trophy for England on 31 July 2022 felt like they had at last reached the pinnacle. It was fitting – a home tournament coupled with a set of performances that was confident yet without their moments of struggle to make the win feel hard-earned and well-deserved.

Each game painted part of the final tapestry that the Lionesses ultimately wanted to portray to the continent and the world.

Setting the tone was vital and an opening match against Austria presented them with a challenge to meet the lofty expectations set after a year of positivity and cautious optimism. We saw what the Lionesses were about in friendlies, but how they fared under the lights was a real test of character. The 1-0 win wasn't spectacular, but it was a much-needed, resolute performance that did indeed set the tone for the rest of the tournament. Trailing Spain for over 60 minutes before making a famous comeback showed persistence in a quarter-final where things could have very easily gone awry.

Narrowly avoiding early setbacks against Sweden before thrashing them 4-0 in the semi-final showed great strength against adversity, once again taking England to another level in their development. The final against Germany was their toughest test yet, coming up against a side that looked incrementally better with each display and looked to peak at Wembley. Yet England's win and game management in extra time was picture-perfect and summed up their desire to win and finish the journey they started all those months ago in September.

We learned from each of these games that the Lionesses and Wiegman changed how they were perceived. The days of Mark Sampson and Hope Powell were when England started to ascertain the mould of a world-class team, but it really took shape under Phil Neville, reaching a World Cup semi-final. Even that era eventually felt quite weary and required a deeper reach to extract more from this generation of players. The introduction of Wiegman has been sensational and the effects are beyond anyone's imagination. What they do from this point on will be compared to their accomplishments of the summer of 2022 as these achievements will forever be immortalised in English sporting folklore.

Looking ahead to the summer of 2023, the World Cup turnaround is quicker than it's ever been and it will need England and Wiegman to tactically innovate and ensure their focus is purely on the next tournament. Tougher tests await the European champions and in the teams of the United States, France, Germany, Spain, and Sweden will they once again face accomplished foes, but they will now go in as equals – if not favourites – in these match-ups. Gone are the days of close calls and 'slight favourites'. What we see now is a new age in the English footballing institution and most importantly, their impact has delivered at long last a vital contribution to their nation.

A hope restored.